Donna Meurrее

⇒ BY WAY OF THE DESERT

365 DAILY READINGS

≫ BY WAY OF THE DESERT

COMPILED AND MODERNIZED BY

BERNARD BANGLEY

PARACLETE PRESS
BREWSTER, MA

By Way of the Desert: 365 Daily Readings

2007 First Printing

Copyright © 2007 by Bernard Bangley

ISBN: 978-1-55725-537-2

Library of Congress Cataloging-in-Publication Data

By way of the desert : 365 daily readings / compiled and modernized by Bernard Bangley.

   p. cm.

  ISBN 978-1-55725-537-2

  1. Devotional calendars. 2. Desert Fathers. I. Bangley, Bernard, 1935-

  BV4810.B9 2007

  242'.2--dc22   2007024342

10 9 8 7 6 5 4 3 2 1

Published by Paraclete Press
Brewster, Massachusetts
www.paracletepress.com

Printed in the United States of America

THE FERTILE CRESCENT is never far from desert wilderness, and the biblical story unfolds among a people familiar with dry sand and hot sun. Throughout the Bible, great spiritual decisions resulted from encounters with God in this silent wilderness.

It was in the desert that Jesus began his public ministry with forty days of retreat. After his baptism by desert-dwelling John, Jesus wisely sought uninterrupted time alone with his heavenly Father. Subjected to powerful temptations, Jesus emerged from his wilderness experience not only with a clear understanding of his assignment, but also with the strength to accomplish it.

Other people of the desert include Elijah, who discovered that God spoke not in the noisy earthquake, wind, and fire, but with "a still, small voice," a voice he detected as he was in the desert hiding from Jezebel.

The experience of those ammas, abbas, monks, nuns, and solitaries who left the world in order to seek God quietly continues a grand biblical precedent. Not only John the Baptist and Elijah, but David also escaped to the desert, avoiding the wrath of King Saul. There can be little doubt that he conceived the substance of many of his psalms in that lonely place.

Nations as well as individuals sought the clarity of the desert. Here, in this arid land, the Israelites wandered with Moses for the span of an entire generation looking to God to lead them. The experience transformed them spiritually.

Abraham, the father of the wandering nation, as we observe near the beginning of the biblical drama, lived his own nomadic life in the desert until God had prepared him for his destiny.

The desert, then, is a place where one's relationship with God may become vivid and inspiring. This severe landscape beckoned alluringly to Christian men and women during the declining years of the Roman Empire. By the fourth century, thousands of Christians lived in the desert areas spanning hundreds of miles on both sides of the Nile, from Egypt to Syria. We may never fully understand what forces motivated them to seek an ascetic life. Yet from their comments, we conclude they sought a purer spirituality than they could find among the distractions of ordinary life. Placing ultimate trust in God, they took extraordinary risks to live in areas wild and barren of resources.

In the book *Lives of the Desert Fathers*, we read about a place in Egypt called Cellia, because of the many hermit cells that were scattered about the desert there. "Those who have already begun their training in Nitria and want to live a more remote life, stripped of external things, withdraw there. For this is the utter desert and the cells are divided from one another by so great a distance that no one can see his neighbor, nor can any voice be heard." Living alone in their cells, the hermits experienced "a huge silence and a great quiet." Only on weekends would these reclusive monastics see each other, in order to receive Holy Communion and worship at church with others in their spiritual community. A fascinating article with photographs may be found on the Internet at www. touregypt.net/featurestories/kellia.htm.

These Christian hermits and monks came from regular occupations in common life. Many were illiterate, and few had any religious training. The more experienced of them attracted followers seeking spiritual direction. Their followers addressed them as "abba" (father), "amma" (mother), and sometimes simply as "old man" or "old woman." These were not official titles, but designations of high regard. A few among these hermits became famous and, to their own dismay, drew many visitors from far away. St. Antony's cave remains a popular tourist destination, as is the monastery of St. Catherine's at Mount Sinai.

Living in a desert freed a person to ponder basic spiritual issues with extended prayer and meditation. While survival required time and attention, there were many quiet, unmolested hours. Monks, nuns, and solitaries explored their personal inner space. It is their recorded insights (some of which are gathered in this collection) that began our rich heritage of Christian mysticism. Centuries later, Meister Eckhart and many others received spiritual direction from these early seekers.

The original texts of these desert writings are in Coptic, Greek, and Syriac. Most of the remarks and anecdotes began as oral tradition and evolved over time into a mixture of legend, quote, and sources unknown that makes a scholar's work difficult. Many sayings remain anonymous, while others may be attributed to several speakers. By medieval times, a Latin translation, *Verba Seniorum*, became the accepted authoritative collection of much of this material.

The selections included in this daily devotional guide represent a wide sampling of the literature associated with the desert fathers and mothers. Within this collection is also a sprinkling of sayings and writings from a few other contemplatives of their time. All have been freshly paraphrased for modern readers. Perhaps, as you read, you will find yourself in contemplation for brief periods in your own personal "desert." Know, then, that you are in the company of men and women for whom the life of the Spirit was the only goal.

Spiritual seekers and disciples of these abbas and ammas often asked for "a word." These short sayings were offered for the listener to reflect upon for long periods of time, until this word of wisdom became an indwelling source of spiritual truth for the seeker.

In order to aid you, the reader, in keeping the essence of the "word" or desert saying in your heart throughout the day, a small portion of the saying or a portion of Scripture upon which it is founded is provided at the end of each daily reading. For the reader who wishes to keep the short phrase in mind, this focus point aids both in remembering the longer "word" throughout the day, and in forming a refrain for meditation, the way various psalms repeat short lines. An example occurs in Psalm 136, where the responsive refrain to every line is "for his steadfast love endures forever."

Here, then, is wisdom from the desert. May the desert offer up spiritual riches for your journey.

➤ BY WAY OF THE DESERT

> *Some judge one day to be better than another,*
> *while others judge all days to be alike.*
> *Let all be fully convinced in their own minds.*
> *Those who observe the day,*
> *observe it in honor of the Lord.*
> ROMANS 14:5–6

ABBA ARSENIUS began to prepare for the glory of Sunday on Saturday evenings. He turned his back to the sun and stretched his hands toward heaven in prayer. He continued this posture all night, until the light of the rising sun struck his face. Then he sat down.

Observe the day in honor of the Lord.

*Our beloved brother Paul
wrote to you according to the
wisdom given him, speaking
of this as he does in all his
letters. There are some things
in them hard to understand.*
2 PETER 3:15–16

ANTONY tested a group that came to visit him by quoting a verse of Scripture. Beginning with the youngest, he asked each for an interpretation. They responded as well as they could, but Antony told them he did not think they understood the verse.

Finally, he turned to Abba Joseph. "How would you explain these words?" Joseph replied, "I do not know."

Antony was elated. "Abba Joseph has found the way, because he admitted he did not know."

**Abba Joseph found the way,
because he admitted he did not know.**

For where your treasure is,
there your heart will be also.
MATTHEW 6:21

A MMA SYNCLETICA said, "We should always be discreet, remaining a part of the community rather than following our own desires. We are exiles from the world. We devote ourselves to faith in God. We have no need of the things we have abandoned. In the world, we had status and a wide variety of food. Here we have a little to eat and not much of anything else."

**For where your treasure is,
there your heart will be also.**

The LORD is good to all,
and his compassion
is over all that he has
made.

PSALM 145:9

ABBA ZENO did not accept any gifts. This hurt the feelings of those who brought him things. Others approached Zeno with a desire for a souvenir of their visit with the old man. Since he had nothing to give them, they also went away disappointed. "What shall I do?" he asked. "The ones who bring things are as troubled as the ones who seek something. I know what I will do. I will accept all gifts and pass these things on to anyone who asks." After adopting this policy, Zeno experienced peace and was able to satisfy all his visitors.

The Lord's compassion
is over all that he has made.

5 JANUARY

The prayer of faith will save the sick, and the LORD will raise
them up; and anyone who has committed sins will be forgiven.
Therefore confess your sins to one another,
and pray for one another, so that you may be healed.
The prayer of the righteous is powerful and effective.
JAMES 5:15–16

AMMA THEODORA taught, "Living in peace is good. Wise people practice continual prayer. Be aware that evil will arrive to burden your soul the moment you determine to live in peace. It will pollute your thoughts and ravage your body with sickness. Evil will weaken both soul and body until you think you cannot pray any more. If we are careful, we can overcome these temptations.

"I know an ascetic who had chills, fevers, and headaches as soon as prayers began. She reasoned, 'I am sick. I am going to die. I will pray before I die.' With this kind of personal motivation, she conquered her sickness and negative thoughts."

Wise people practice continual prayer.

6 JANUARY

You guide me with your counsel,
and afterward you will receive
me with honor. Whom have I
in heaven but you? And there
is nothing on earth that I desire
other than you. My flesh and my heart
> *may fail, but God is the strength of my heart*
> *and my portion forever.*
> PSALM 73:24–26

A BROTHER asked Euprepius, "How does the fear of God live in the soul?" The old man replied, "If you have humility, live in poverty, and do not pass judgment on others, the fear of God will come to you."

God is the strength of my heart
and my portion forever.

It is no longer I who live, but it is Christ who lives in me. And the life I now live in the flesh I live by faith in the Son of God, who loved me and gave himself for me.

GALATIANS 2:20

WHEN SOMEONE asked Abba Antony what activity would please God, he answered, "Follow my instructions. Keep God in your thoughts at all times. Conduct your life after the pattern taught in Holy Scripture. Remain in one location rather than constantly traveling around."

I live by faith in the Son of God.

8 JANUARY

*Martha, Martha, you are worried and distracted by many
things; there is need of only one thing. Mary has chosen the
better part, which will not be taken away from her.*

LUKE 10:41–42

EVAGRIUS spoke intelligently at a meeting. The priest
commented, "Abba, if you lived at home, you would
probably be a leading bishop, but you sit out here in
obscurity." This filled Evagrius with Godly sorrow, but
did not disturb his peace. Bowing slightly, he quoted Job:
"I did speak once or twice, but never again."

There is need of only one thing.

Beloved,
never avenge yourselves,
but leave room for the wrath of
God; for it is written, "Vengeance
is mine, I will repay, says the Lord."

ROMANS 12:19

A BROTHER who had been hurt by another brother visited Sisois of Thebes. He reported his injury and commented that he wanted to get even. The hermit advised him to leave all matters of vengeance in God's hands. The brother refused to drop the matter. "I can't rest until I get even."

Sisois then invited the offended brother to join him in prayer. The hermit stood and prayed, "O God, we don't need you anymore. We can take vengeance ourselves." The brother fell repentantly to the hermit's feet. "I will not continue quarrelling with my brother. Please forgive me."

Beloved, never avenge yourselves.

10 JANUARY

As for what [seeds] fell among the thorns,

these are the ones who hear; but as they go on their way,

they are choked by the cares and riches and pleasures of

life, and their fruit does not mature.

LUKE 8:14

ABBA EUPREPIUS said, "Love of material things sets us up for spiritual failure. Therefore, if you lose something, be grateful. The loss frees you from care."

**If you lose something, be grateful.
The loss frees you from care.**

Not to us, O LORD, not to us, but to your name give glory,
for the sake of your steadfast love and your faithfulness.
PSALM 115:1

JOSEPH OF THEBES said, "God recognizes three honorable things. The first is when someone who is weak accepts temptations with gratitude. The second is behavior that is pure and unadulterated with human motive. The third is when a disciple obeys a spiritual father, surrendering all self-will."

Not to us, O Lord, but to your name give glory.

Sorrow is better than laughter,
for by sadness of countenance
the heart is made glad.

ECCLESIASTES 7:3

AMMA SYNCLETICA said, "There are two kinds of sorrow. One is helpful; the other harmful. Sorrow is helpful when we weep for our sins, and for the ignorance of others. This sorrow will not allow us to become complacent, but instead prods us on toward true goodness. Our spiritual enemy sends sorrow that produces lethargy. This is harmful sorrow, and we need to drive it away with prayers and psalms."

There are two kinds of sorrow.
One is helpful; the other harmful.

God gave them up in the lusts of their hearts to impurity,
to the degrading of their bodies among themselves,
because they exchanged the truth about God for a lie
and worshiped and served the creature
rather than the Creator, who is blessed forever!
ROMANS 1:24–25

ABBA ISAIAH explained that when God takes pity on a rebellious soul, he allows it to experience self-induced suffering, prompting the soul to turn to him again.

God prompts the rebellious soul to turn to him again.

God's kingdom isn't something you can see.
There is no use saying,
"Look! Here it is" or "Look! There it is."
God's kingdom is here with you.
LUKE 17:20–21 CEV

ABBA ANTONY said, "Become familiar with virtue. It is not something that is far from us; neither is it outside us. We have the capacity for virtue and we can have it if we desire it. The Greeks sail across seas to expand their knowledge, but there is no necessity for us to travel for the kingdom of God. We do not need to cross an ocean to find virtue. Our Lord told us the kingdom of God is within us. We possess everything we need to become virtuous."

The kingdom of God is within us.

15 JANUARY

Rejoice always, pray without ceasing, give
thanks in all circumstances; for this is the
will of God in Christ Jesus for you.

1 THESSALONIANS 5:16–18

WHEN THE ABBOT of a monastery told Epiphanius that his Palestinian monks strictly observed prayers at certain hours, Epiphanius replied, "Obviously, you neglect the other hours of the day. Never cease praying. A genuine monk will have prayer and psalms active in his heart all the time."

Rejoice always; pray without ceasing.

16 JANUARY

Divided tongues, as of fire, appeared among them,
and a tongue rested on each of them
[when the Holy Spirit arrived at Pentecost].
ACTS 2:3

ABBA LOT visited Abba Joseph and summarized his religious life this way: "Abba, I recite the liturgy the best I can, sometimes I fast, I pray and meditate, I try to live peacefully with others, and I attempt to cleanse my thoughts. What more can I do?"

The old man Joseph stood up, stretching his hands toward heaven. His fingers seemed to be ten lamps of fire. He said to Lot, "If you will, you can become all flame."

If you will, you can become all flame.

Hide your face from my sins,
and blot out all my iniquities.
Create in me a clean heart, O God,
and put a new and right spirit within me.
Do not cast me away from your presence,
and do not take your holy spirit from me.
Restore to me the joy of your salvation,
and sustain in me a willing spirit.
PSALM 51:9–12

ABBA ELIAS asked, "What can sin accomplish when there is penitence? How can love function when there is pride?"

Create in me a clean heart, O God.

Love your enemies, do good, and lend,

expecting nothing in return. Your reward will be great

and you will be children of the Most High;

for he is kind to the ungrateful and the wicked.

Be merciful, just as your Father is merciful.

LUKE 6:35–36

ABBA ZENO said, "If you want God to hear your prayer quickly, then before you pray for anything else, even your own soul, when you stand and stretch out your hands toward God, pray with all your heart for your enemies. When you do this, God will respect all that you ask."

Be merciful, just as your Father is merciful.

Be strong in the LORD and in the strength of his power.
Put on the whole armor of God,
so that you may be able to stand against the wiles of the devil.
For our struggle is not against enemies of blood and flesh,
but against the rulers, against the authorities,
against the cosmic powers of this present darkness,
against the spiritual forces of evil in the heavenly places.
Therefore take up the whole armor of God,
so that you may be able to withstand on that evil day,
and having done everything, to stand firm.
EPHESIANS 6:10–13

AMMA SYNCLETICA said, "The best athletes must compete with stronger opponents."

Be strong in the Lord.

Whenever you face trials of any kind,
consider it nothing but joy,
because you know that the testing
of your faith produces endurance;
and let endurance have its full effect,
so that you may be mature and complete,
lacking in nothing.
JAMES 1:2–4

OTHERS report that Amma Sarah struggled against sexual temptation for thirteen years. She never prayed that the spiritual warfare should end. Instead, she prayed, "God, give me strength."

The testing of your faith produces endurance.

The steadfast love of the LORD
is from everlasting to everlasting
on those who fear him.

PSALM 103:17

A SOLDIER asked Abba Milos if God would forgive a sinner. After teaching him carefully, Milos said, "Tell me, young man, if you rip your cloak will you throw it away?"

"No, of course not."

"Then, if you care that much about your cloak, do you not expect God to have mercy on his creature?"

The steadfast love of the Lord is everlasting.

22 JANUARY

Even if you say to this mountain,
"Be lifted up and thrown into the sea,"
it will be done. Whatever you ask for in
prayer with faith, you will receive.

MATTHEW 21:21–22

WHEN A BROTHER asked Abba Antony to pray for him, the old man replied, "Try to pray your own prayers."

Whatever you ask for in prayer with faith, you will receive.

Do not neglect to show hospitality to strangers, for by doing
that some have entertained angels without knowing it.
HEBREWS 13:2

ON HIS WAY INTO TOWN, ABBA AGATHON met a
cripple with paralyzed legs beside the road. The
cripple called out, "Where are you going?"

"Into town to sell some things."

The cripple pleaded, "Please carry me there."

Agathon agreed to help him. In town, he put the invalid
on the ground beside him and began to offer his things
for sale. When the first sale was completed, his new
companion asked, "What was the price of that item?"
Agathon told him, and he responded, "Buy me a cake."
Agathon complied.

When he sold a second item, the invalid asked the
same question about price. When told, he made another
request for a purchase. This continued until Agathon had
sold everything that he brought into town.

"Are you ready to return?" asked the cripple.

"Yes."

"Then please carry me back to the place where you found me."

Again Abba Agathon picked him up and carried him.

The invalid then said, "Agathon, you are filled with the blessing of God, in heaven and on earth." Turning in his direction, Agathon saw no one. Agathon perceived he had carried an angel of the Lord.

Do not neglect to show hospitality to strangers.

I say this for your own benefit,
not to put any restraint upon you,
but to promote good order
and unhindered devotion to the Lord.
1 CORINTHIANS 7:35

ABBA EVAGRIUS told us that praying without distraction is wonderful, but chanting psalms without distraction is superior.

Seek good order and unhindered devotion.

25 JANUARY

Do not let the sun go down on your anger.
EPHESIANS 4:26

ABBA AGATHON said, "I have never gone to sleep with a grievance against anyone, and as far as possible, I have never let anyone go to sleep with a grievance against me."

Do not let the sun go down on your anger.

26 JANUARY

The LORD God says, "I will pour out my spirit on all flesh;
your sons and your daughters shall prophesy,
your old men shall dream dreams,
and your young men shall see visions."
JOEL 2:28

ABBA OLYMPIOS taught this lesson: A pagan priest visited Scetis, came to my cell, and slept there. Considering the monks' pattern of life, he asked me, "Living like this, do you receive spiritual visions?"

I answered, "No."

He said to me, "When we make a sacrifice to our god, he grants us insights into mysteries, but you who are dedicated to extreme hardship, vigils, prayers, and asceticism, report seeing nothing. If you see nothing, it is because you have impure thoughts in your hearts which separate you from your God."

I reported his words to the monks. They respected the pagan priest and agreed that he was correct.

Impure thoughts separate us from God.

For everything there is a season and a time
for every matter under heaven.
A time to keep silence, and a time to speak.
ECCLESIASTES 3:1, 7B

A S A BEGINNER, EUPREPIUS visited an old man and asked, "Abba, tell me what is important." He answered, "When you call on someone, do not speak until you are spoken to." Stung by the comment, Euprepius bowed and said, "Nothing like this teaching is in any of the many books I have read." Saying this, Euprepius departed with greater understanding.

There is a time to keep silence,
and a time to speak.

*If there is any excellence and if there is anything
worthy of praise, think about these things.*
PHILIPPIANS 4:8

JOHN THE DWARF said, "I can imagine someone embodying all Christian virtues. Rising every morning at dawn, he would begin immediately to keep God's commandments. He would be patient, reverent, and selfless in God's love. With genuine humility, he would control soul and body. He would pray regularly and sincerely. Injury would not upset him. This virtuous person would never consider revenge and retaliation. He would not attempt to inflate his ego by criticizing others. He would live in lowliness of spirit, as one crucified. While using discretion, he would resist evil. His hands would be busy with work, and he would not complain of deprivation. He would sense the nearness of death."

**If there is anything worthy of praise,
think about these things.**

29 JANUARY

*Those with good sense are slow to anger, and it
is their glory to overlook an offense.*

PROVERBS 19:11

ABBA AMMONAS remarked, "I have asked God night and day for fourteen years to give me victory over anger."

Those with good sense are slow to anger.

*I commend enjoyment, for there is nothing better for people
under the sun than to eat, and drink, and enjoy themselves,
for this will go with them in their toil through the days of life
that God gives them under the sun.*

ECCLESIASTES 8:15

A DESERT HUNTER saw Abba Antony having fun with
the brothers. He was shocked and expressed his
dismay because of their frivolity. The old man said to the
hunter, "Put an arrow in your bow and shoot it." When
he did so, Antony said, "Now shoot another." Again, the
hunter complied.

Then the old man asked him to shoot a third arrow. The
hunter hesitated. "If I bend my bow too many times, I will
weaken and break it."

Antony said to him, "It is the same with God's work. If
we stretch the brothers beyond measure, they will weaken
and break."

**If we stretch ourselves beyond measure,
we will weaken and break.**

3 I JANUARY

He gives snow like wool; he scatters frost like
ashes. He hurls down hail like crumbs—
who can stand before his cold?

PSALM 147:16–17

AMMA THEODORA said, "Let us strive to enter by the narrow gate. In the same way that trees will not bear fruit until they have stood the storms of winter, so it is with us. This present time is a storm. It is only through the experience of the many difficulties and temptations of our days that we will enter the kingdom of heaven."

**They bear no fruit until they have
stood the storms of winter.**

For by the grace given to me I say to everyone among you not
to think of yourself more highly than you ought to think,
but to think with sober judgment,
each according to the measure of faith
that God has assigned.
ROMANS 12:3

ABBA ANTONY said, "I saw all the snares that the enemy scatters all over the world. Groaning, I asked, 'What can get through these traps?' Then I heard a voice speaking to me, 'Humility.'"

Think with sober judgment.

2 FEBRUARY

The gifts he gave were that some would be apostles,
some prophets, some evangelists, some pastors
and teachers, to equip the saints for the work of
ministry, for building up the body of Christ.
EPHESIANS 4:11–12

A BROTHER asked a hermit to tell him the proper thing to do with his life. The hermit replied that only God knows what is good, but that the great Nesteros, a friend of Antony, made a strong point when he said, "God is equally pleased by all good works. Scripture tells us that Abraham was hospitable and God was with him. Elijah sought quiet and God was with him. David had humility and God was with him. Therefore, whatever attracts you in the service of God is good. Do it, and let your heart be at peace."

Whatever attracts you
in the service of God is good.

After Jesus had left that place,
he passed along the Sea of Galilee,
and he went up the mountain,
where he sat down.
MATTHEW 15:29

ANTONY THE GREAT said, "In the same way that fish will die if they remain out of water, monks who linger outside their cells or socialize too much diminish the force of their inner peace."

**Those who socialize too much
diminish the force of their inner peace.**

Those who belong to Christ Jesus
have crucified the flesh
with its passions and desires.

GALATIANS 5:24

ABBA MACARIUS made a rule for himself regarding eating with the brothers. He decided that if they offered him wine, he would accept it graciously, but for each cup of wine he would deny himself water for a day. When some of the brothers wanted to refresh him with a cup of wine, he took it joyfully, seizing an opportunity to deny himself. His student understood what was involved and said to the brothers, "Please, for God's sake, don't offer him any wine. He will pay for it in the privacy of his cell." Thereafter, the brothers offered Macarius no more wine.

Those who belong to Christ Jesus
have crucified the flesh.

5 FEBRUARY

Every species of beast and bird, of reptile and sea creature,
can be tamed by the human species, but no one can tame the
tongue—a restless evil, full of deadly poison.
JAMES 3:7–8

A BBA SISOIS was confident that for thirty years he had sinned every time he prayed. "When I pray, I ask the Lord Jesus Christ to protect me from my tongue, but my tongue continues to make me stumble every day."

When I pray, I ask the Lord
to protect me from my tongue.

6 FEBRUARY

Should a multitude of words go unanswered,
and should one full of talk be vindicated?
JOB 11:2

A BROTHER, in conversation with Abba Theodore, talked about religious matters beyond his personal experience. Theodore commented, "You are looking for a ship, but you have not found one. You have not put your luggage on board, and you have not put out to sea. But as you talk with me, you seem already to be at the city you intend to reach. If you make some effort to do the things you talk about, then you can discuss them with comprehension."

Make some effort to do the things you talk about.

They inquired again of the LORD.
  1 SAMUEL 10:22

A BROTHER approached a hermit and said, "Abba, I ask my elders questions. They give me excellent spiritual guidance, but then I can't remember what they said. Is there any value in asking questions when I don't retain the answers?"

The hermit gestured toward two empty bottles. "Take one of those bottles and fill it with oil. Rinse it, pour it out, and return it to me." When he had followed these directions, the hermit instructed him to do it a few more times.

"Now examine both containers and tell me which is cleanest."

The brother answered, "The one that held the oil."

"That's the way it works for a person who asks questions. Even though you may not recall the answers, your soul will be cleaner than if you had not asked any questions."

Inquire again of the Lord.

8 FEBRUARY

Do not boast about tomorrow,
for you do not know
what a day may bring.
     PROVERBS 27:1

MACARIUS THE GREAT said, "You should live as though you might die tomorrow, but at the same time treat your body as though you will live for many more years. The first thought will eliminate every trace of torpor, letting you be more fervent, and the second will maintain good health."

Do not boast about tomorrow.

> *I will pray with the spirit, but I will pray*
> *with the mind also; I will sing praise with the spirit,*
> *but I will sing praise with the mind also.*
> 1 CORINTHIANS 14:15

EVAGRIUS PONTICUS wrote that you will not always be able to follow every detail of your rule of life, but you should do the best you can to whatever limited degree. Demons will be eager to seize their opportunity. They will try to prevent us from attempting any part of what seems like an impossible chore. They keep the sick from offering prayers of thanks while in pain. They will destroy your patience. They encourage fasting on those who are already weak. They prompt a sick person to sing for long periods while standing on trembling legs.

I will pray with the spirit,
but I will pray with the mind also.

I have found the book of the law
in the house of the LORD.
2 KINGS 22:8

E PIPHANIUS said, "It is important to acquire Christian books. The very sight of them on the shelf will make you more likely to avoid sin. They encourage us to put more value on righteousness."

I have found the book
of the law in the house of the Lord.

> *Beware of practicing your piety before others in*
> *order to be seen by them; for then you have no*
> *reward from your Father in heaven.*
> MATTHEW 6:1

A HERMIT who was fasting visited another hermit. While they were together, other pilgrims also visited. The hermit cooked them a little vegetable soup. When they sat down for the meal, the fasting hermit dipped a single pea in the soup and slowly chewed it. After supper, the host hermit took his fasting visitor aside and said, "Brother, when you visit someone, don't make a show of your way of life. If you want to keep your personal rule, remain in your cell." The brother accepted this advice. From then on, he behaved as the others and ate what his host served.

Beware of practicing your piety before others.

*A young man named Eutychus, who was sitting
in the window, began to sink off into a deep sleep
while Paul talked still longer.* ACTS 20:9

CASSIAN told about a desert hermit who prayed that he would not fall asleep during any beneficial conversation. On the other hand, he asked God to allow him to doze whenever someone should speak hateful words that he did not want to hear. He said small talk has a wider appeal than spiritual instruction. He reported that once when he was having a religious discussion with some brothers they became drowsy and nodded off to sleep. "I wanted to demonstrate that this was the devil's work. I began to gossip and they came out of their slumber and paid rapt attention. I told them when we were talking about heaven they drifted off to sleep, but the moment I began frivolous comments they eagerly listened. I pointed out this was the devil's activity and urged them to stay awake when spiritual things are being discussed."

Stay awake.

13 FEBRUARY

Do not judge, so that you may not be judged. For with the judgment you make you will be judged, and the measure you give will be the measure you get. Why do you see the speck in your neighbor's eye, but do not notice the log in your own eye?

MATTHEW 7:1–3

A BROTHER approached a hermit and told him that two monks were living together in a homosexual relationship. The hermit was certain a demon was misleading the brother and summoned the two monks. That night he prepared a pallet where they could sleep together and gave them one blanket. The hermit commented, "They are sons of God, holy persons." Then the hermit instructed a disciple to send the slanderer to a cell by himself. "He is a victim of the very thing he projects on them."

Do not judge, so that you may not be judged.

Your proud heart has deceived you.
OBADIAH 1:3

A MMA SYNCLETICA said, "For those who live in monasteries, obedience is superior to chastity. This is because chastity may lead to pride, while obedience may promote humility."

Obedience is superior to chastity.

*Set the believers an example in speech and conduct,
in love, in faith, in purity.* 1 TIMOTHY 4:12

ABBA ANTONY quietly advised those who visited him
to turn their backs on the praise of the world and
seek the joy of a hermitage. If others who were more
powerful were oppressing any of his visitors, he vigorously
defended them as though he were experiencing injustice
vicariously. His comments were valuable to many. Some
gave away their riches and eagerly followed Antony's way
of life. We can characterize this man by saying that, in
him, Christ gave the desert an outstanding doctor.

Sadness turned to joy in Abba Antony's presence. Anger
became serenity. Merely the sight of Antony comforted the
grieving. Those who were looking back to a more comfortable
life reaffirmed their commitment to poverty. He restored
waning enthusiasm for the hermit's life. Young men, burning
with desire, would rededicate themselves to chastity after
time with Antony. He exorcised demons. People who were
utterly confused would return home composed and at peace.

**Set the believers an example in speech
and conduct.**

Every sword was against the other,
so that there was very great confusion. 1 SAMUEL 14:20

THREE FRIENDS attempted Christian living in different ways. The first wanted to be a peacemaker who could reconcile opponents. The second decided to visit the sick. The third departed for the desert where he could live in quiet and prayer.

The first was not able to settle many disputes. Discouraged, he went to the friend who was visiting the sick and found him discouraged as well. Both of them journeyed out into the desert to visit the one who was quietly praying. They told him their difficulties in attempting to live a Christian life.

After being silent for a while, the third friend then poured water into a bowl and asked them to examine it. The pouring had stirred up sediment. Later, he asked them to look at the water again. Now it had settled clear and they could look at their reflections in it. He explained, "This is the way it is for those who live among others. Commotion keeps them from seeing clearly."

Commotion keeps us from seeing clearly.

17 FEBRUARY

*[Jesus] told them a parable: "No one tears a piece from a
new garment and sews it on an old garment; otherwise the
new will be torn, and the piece from the new will not match
the old. And no one puts new wine into old wineskins;
otherwise the new wine will burst the skins and will be spilled,
and the skins will be destroyed. But new wine must be put into
fresh wineskins. And no one after drinking old wine desires
new wine, but says, 'The old is good.'"*

Luke 5:36–39

Abba Poemen said Abba Pior made a fresh start
every morning.

New wine must be put into fresh wineskins.

I have swept away your transgressions like a cloud, and your sins like mist; return to me, for I have redeemed you.

ISAIAH 44:22

ABBA MACARIUS THE GREAT showed mercy even as God is merciful. Macarius ignored the faults of others as though he never observed them. When someone spoke of the sins of others, Macarius did not hear.

Return to me, for I have redeemed you.

Give instruction to the wise, and they will become wiser still;
teach the righteous and they will gain in learning.
PROVERBS 9:9

LONGINUS told Abba Lucius, "There are three things I want to do. The first is to go on a pilgrimage."

Lucius answered, "Unless you control your tongue, you will never be a pilgrim no matter how far you travel. If you control your tongue here, you will be a pilgrim without going anywhere."

Longinus continued, "My second idea is to fast two days at a time."

Lucius responded, "The prophet Isaiah asked, 'Is such the fast that I choose, a day to humble oneself? Is it to bow down the head like a bulrush, and to lie in sackcloth and ashes? Will you call this a fast, a day acceptable to the Lord?' (Isaiah 58:5). It would be better if you guarded your mind from evil thoughts."

Longinus said, "My third idea is to avoid the company of others."

Lucius replied, "The important thing is to deal with your sins while living among others. Otherwise, you will not be able to deal with yourself when you live alone."

**Teach the righteous
and they will gain in learning.**

*We who are strong ought to put up with the failings of
the weak, and not to please ourselves. Each of us must
please our neighbor for the good purpose of
building up the neighbor.*
ROMANS 15:1–2

ABBA ANTONY said, "Our life and death depend upon
our relationship with our neighbor. If we gain our
neighbor, we have gained God. If we offend our neighbor,
we have sinned against Christ."

If we gain our neighbor, we have gained God.

If you, O LORD, should mark iniquities,
LORD, who could stand?
PSALM 130:3

ABBA POEMEN received a brother who said, "I am deeply disturbed and I want to leave here."

"Why?"

"Because I have heard a distressing tale about one of the brothers."

"Is it true?"

"Yes, abba. The brother who told me is trustworthy."

Abba Poemen did not agree. "The one who told you that story is not reliable. If he were, he never would have passed it on to you. When God heard cries from Sodom, he did not believe it until he had gone down and seen it with his own eyes."

"But I have seen the story confirmed with my own eyes."

Hearing this, Poemen reached down and picked up a piece of straw. "What is this?" he asked.

"A straw."

Reaching up to the ceiling, he asked, "And what is this?"

"The beam that supports the roof."

Then Poemen said, "Remember that your sins are like this beam while your brother's sins are like this straw."

Hearing this, the formerly outraged brother was stunned. "How shall I ever thank you, Abba Poemen? Your teaching is like precious jewelry, full of God's grace and glory."

**If you, O Lord, should mark iniquities,
Lord, who could stand?**

Who are you to pass judgment on servants of another?
It is before their own lord that they stand or fall. And they
will be upheld, for the Lord is able to make them stand.

ROMANS 14:4

ABBA MOSES hesitated to accept a summons to be part of a council that would pass judgment on a brother who had committed a sin. A delegation approached him insisting that all the others were waiting for him. Reluctantly, he got up and went with them. He took a jug of water that leaked all along the path.

The council came outside to greet him. Puzzled by the water jug, they asked for an explanation. Moses said, "My sins pour out behind me, and I have the audacity to come here today to judge someone else's errors."

Hearing this, they forgave the sinful brother and sent him on his way.

My sins pour out behind me.

*For [God] makes his sun rise on the evil and on the good, and
sends rain on the righteous and on the unrighteous.*

MATTHEW 5:45

JOHN CLIMACUS wrote, "Every free creature lives in God. God is everyone's salvation. God loves believers and unbelievers, the just and the unjust, the pious and the secular, those free of passions and those subject to passions, monks and those living worldly lives, the educated and the illiterate, the healthy and the sick, the young and the old. God is like an outpouring of light, a glimpse of the sun, or changes in the weather. God touches everyone, without exception, through these things."

Every free creature lives in God.

Teach me, and I will be silent; make me
understand how I have gone wrong.
How forceful are honest words! But your
reproof, what does it reprove?
JOB 6:24–25

ABBA PAUL the Barber and his brother Timothy frequently argued with each other. One day, Abba Paul asked, "How long shall we continue to argue like this?"

Abba Timothy had an idea. "From now on, you take my side of an argument, and I will take your side." They did this for the remainder of their lives.

Make me understand how I have gone wrong.

> *You shall love your neighbor as yourself:*
> *I am the LORD.*
> LEVITICUS 19:18

T WO BROTHERS visited Abba Pambo. One of them said, "Abba, I fast two days, and then I eat two large buns. Do you think I am doing the right thing?" The other brother said, "I prepare two vegetable stews every day. I keep a little for myself, and give the remainder to the needy. Am I doing the proper thing?" They urged him to answer, but Abba Pambo remained silent.

After several days without any response, the brothers became discouraged. They considered it useless to wait any longer for some word from Pambo, and began to prepare for departure. The clergy encouraged them to wait a little longer. "It's always like this with the abba. He remains silent until God gives him something to say."

The brothers returned to Abba Pambo and said, "Abba, pray for us."

"Are you ready to leave?"

"Yes."

He studied them, imagining himself in their place. Writing on the ground, he said, "Pambo fasts two days and then eats two large buns. Does this behavior make him a monk? No, it does not."

Continuing, he said, "Pambo makes two vegetable stews every day and gives them to the poor. Do you think this makes him a monk? Not at all."

He fell silent for a while before speaking again. "These are both good works, but the way to be saved is to behave correctly toward your neighbor."

The brothers were encouraged, and returned home pleased.

Love your neighbor as yourself.

> *For [God's] anger is but for a moment; his favor*
> *is for a lifetime. Weeping may linger for the*
> *night, but joy comes with the morning.*
> PSALM 30:5

AMMA SYNCLETICA said, "Anger is not good. If you become angry, do not allow it to remain with you all day."

Do not allow anger to remain with you all day.

27 FEBRUARY

Keep your heart with all vigilance,
for from it flow the springs of life.
PROVERBS 4:23

ABBA ANTONY said, "When you sit quietly alone you escape three wars: hearing, speaking, and seeing. The one thing you will fight all the time is your own heart."

Keep your heart with all vigilance.

The LORD was with Joseph, and he became a successful man;
he was in the house of his Egyptian master. His master saw
that the LORD was with him, and that the LORD caused all
that he did to prosper in his hands. So Joseph found favor
in his sight and attended him; he made him overseer of
his house and put him in charge of all that he had.
GENESIS 39:2–4

ABBA ORSISIUS said, "If you use unbaked brick to build a house near a river, it will quickly collapse. Baked brick becomes like stone. In the same way, those who are wise to the ways of the world, but know nothing of the word of God, are vulnerable. Living among others subjects us to constant temptation.

"It is important for you to realize your weakness early. Do not attempt to carry too heavy a burden. Once your faith is strong, you will be secure. Read about Joseph in the Old Testament. He suffered dreadful temptations in Egypt where people neglected worship of God. But God was with Joseph, protecting him through every trial. Admit your weakness and continue the struggle."

Admit your weakness and continue the struggle.

Do all things without murmuring and arguing, so that you
may be blameless and innocent, children of God without
blemish in the midst of a crooked and perverse generation,
in which you shine like stars in the world.

PHILIPPIANS 2:14–15

A BROTHER asked a hermit to tell him one thing that would guide his life. The hermit answered, "When you are able to accept injury, enduring it without complaint, this will be a great thing. It is at the top of the list of virtues."

Do all things without murmuring and arguing.

You have instructed many; you have strengthened the weak hands. Your words have supported those who were stumbling, and you have made firm the feeble knees.

JOB 4:3–4

CASSIAN relates this about Abba John, who led a community because of his outstanding life. When John was on his deathbed, he remained cheerful and thought about his Lord. The brothers who stood around him requested that he make a statement that would summarize the way to salvation. They wanted it as an inheritance that would guide them in their own life in Christ. Sighing, John said, "I have never given in to my own desires, and I never asked anyone else to do something I did not do myself."

Your words have supported those who were stumbling.

> *Glory in his holy name; let the hearts of those*
> *who seek the LORD rejoice. Seek the LORD*
> *and his strength, seek his presence continually.*
> 1 CHRONICLES 16:10–11

ANTONY THE GREAT watched another hermit sitting at his work, rising to pray, sitting down again and plaiting a rope, then getting up to pray. An angel spoke to Antony, "Do this and you will be saved." These words filled him with joy and courage.

Seek God's presence continually.

Then they brought to him a demoniac who was blind
and mute; and he cured him, so that the one who had
been mute could speak and see. All the crowds were
amazed and said, "Can this be the Son of David?"
But when the Pharisees heard it, they said, "It is only
by Beelzebul, the ruler of the demons, that this fellow
casts out the demons."
MATTHEW 12:22–24

ABBA ISAIAH said, "The most helpful thing for a beginner in prayer is insults. The neophyte who regularly bears insults is like a tree planted by water."

**The one who bears insults
is like a tree planted by water.**

Then [Jesus] withdrew from them about a stone's throw, knelt down, and prayed, "Father if you are willing, remove this cup from me; yet, not my will but yours be done." Then an angel from heaven appeared to him and gave him strength. In his anguish he prayed more earnestly, and his sweat became like great drops of blood falling down on the ground.

LUKE 22:41–44

SOME BROTHERS asked Agathon which good work required the most effort. He replied, "No labor is more difficult than prayer. Demons understand that prayer is a path to God. They will do everything possible to hinder this journey. Prayer is like fighting a war."

Prayer is a path to God.

5 MARCH

Let even those who have wives be as though
they had none, and those who mourn as though
they were not mourning, and those who rejoice
as though they were not rejoicing, and those
who buy as though they had no possessions, and
those who deal with the world
as though they had no dealings with it.
1 CORINTHIANS 7:29–31

ABBA ZOSIMAS remembered a brother who had some vegetables and said, "He planted seed and cultivated the plants. While he did not pull them up or throw them away, he possessed his vegetables as though he did not actually own them. That's why he was not troubled when his elder tested him by destroying them. He acted as though it was of no importance. When only one root remained, he said, 'Abba, if it pleases you, leave that one so we may share a meal.' It became clear that the elder's disciple served God and not his vegetables."

Deal with the world
as though you have no dealings with it.

6 MARCH

Clothe yourselves with humility in your
dealings with one another.
1 PETER 5:5

WHEN ABBA ARSENIUS lived in the Emperor's palace, he became the best-dressed person in the court. When he began to live as a monk, no one wore clothes that were more ragged.

Be clothed with humility.

They sent Barnabas to Antioch. When he came and saw the
grace of God, he rejoiced, and he exhorted them all to remain
faithful to the LORD with steadfast devotion; for he was a good
man, full of the Holy Spirit and of faith.

ACTS 11:22–24

ABBA ARSENIUS avoided discussion of the Scripture, even though he was an excellent expositor. He was also reluctant to write letters to anyone. When he attended public worship, he sat behind a pillar to prevent himself or others from being distracted.

Remain faithful to the Lord.

> *Let all who take refuge in you rejoice;*
> *let them ever sing for joy.*
> *Spread your protection over them,*
> *so that those who love your name may exult in you.*
>
> PSALM 5:11

ON THE MOUNTAIN OF ANTONY, seven monks took turns chasing away the birds when the grape harvest approached. When one of them took his turn guarding the grapes, he would shout, "Go away, bad thoughts inside, bad birds outside!"

Let all who take refuge in you rejoice.

9 MARCH

When words are many, transgression is not lacking,
but the prudent are restrained in speech.

PROVERBS 10:19

ABBA AMMONAS said, "Scrutinize yourself carefully. Then if anyone harms you in any way, you will remain silent. You will not say anything at all until constant prayer has softened your heart. Later, you will be able to console the one who offended you."

The prudent restrain their speech.

*Do not be wise
in your own eyes;
fear the LORD,
and turn away from evil.*
PROVERBS 3:7

AN EGYPTIAN HERMIT said, "When you begin to feel a sense of pride or vanity, examine your conscience. Are you keeping God's commandments? Do you love your enemies? Are you glad when your enemy triumphs and saddened by his downfall? Do you recognize that you are an unfaithful servant and the chief of sinners? When you have searched your heart, do not then think that you have corrected all your faults. To do so would be to destroy all the good you have accomplished."

Do not be wise in your own eyes.

Look on my right hand and see—
there is no one who takes notice of me;
no refuge remains to me;
no one cares for me.
PSALM 142:4

EVAGRIUS PONTICIUS wrote, "Apathy (*acedia*) seriously damages the soul. Indifference attacks us most strenuously during the middle of the day. A sense of dreariness makes us think that time is creeping by. Bored, we think a day lasts fifty hours. In torpor, we step outside and try to observe some movement of the sun. We begin to hate where we are, hate life itself, and hate manual labor. We think no one cares and no one can encourage us. The slightest offense becomes unbearable.

"Indifference to your present circumstances leads you to look for other places where you can live more comfortably and be successful in business. Rationalizing, you believe that pleasing the Lord has nothing to do with this place. You are convinced God can be loved everywhere. This cruel demon leads you to think how this present dreariness will stretch into the distant future. It will stop at nothing in its effort to prompt you to forsake your cell and drop out of the fight.

None of the other demons will press you as hard as this one, never giving up. The struggle against it will fill you with unfathomable peace and indescribable joy."

Apathy seriously damages the soul.

A gentle tongue is a tree of life,
but perverseness
in it breaks the spirit.
PROVERBS I5:4

BROTHER JOHN KLIMAKOS said, "When you finish your prayers, restrain your tongue. The tongue is capable of quickly dispersing what you have worked to gather."

A gentle tongue is a tree of life.

13 MARCH

Woe to you, scribes and Pharisees,
hypocrites! For you clean
the outside of the cup and
of the plate, but inside
they are full of greed and
self-indulgence. You blind
Pharisee! First clean the
inside of the cup, so that the
outside also may become clean.
MATTHEW 23:25–26

ABBA ARSENIUS said, "Try as hard as you can to align your inner activity with God. This will allow you to defeat exterior passions."

First clean the inside of the cup.

> *Two others also, who were criminals,*
> *were led away to be put to death with him.*
> *When they came to the place that is called The Skull,*
> *they crucified Jesus there with the criminals,*
> *one on his right and one on his left. Then Jesus said,*
> *"Father, forgive them; for they do not know*
> *what they are doing."*
> LUKE 23:32–34

ABBA ZENO told us, "If you want God to hear your prayer when you stand, stretching out your hands toward God, you must sincerely begin by praying for your enemies. When you do this, God will respect all you request."

Begin by praying for your enemies.

15 MARCH

Now listen to me.
I will give you counsel,
and God be with you!

EXODUS 18:19

A BROTHER visited Abba Moses to ask his advice. Moses told him, "Go and sit alone in your cell. Your cell will teach you everything."

Your cell will teach you everything.

*Right away he follows her, and goes like an ox to the slaughter,
or bounds like a stag toward the trap until an arrow pierces its
entrails. He is like a bird rushing into a snare, not knowing
that it will cost him his life.*

PROVERBS 7:22–23

A BROTHER who was obsessed with lust got out of bed one night and went to a hermit to talk about his temptations. The hermit counseled him and he returned to his cell. Lustful temptations returned and he visited the hermit a second time. This pattern continued for some time.

The hermit never reprimanded him, but spoke these helpful words: "Never submit to the devil. Be careful about your soul. When this demon disturbs you, come to me and I will rebuke him. He will leave you alone. Nothing disturbs lust more than exposing its urgings. Nothing helps it more than hiding the temptations."

After the brother complained about his problem to the hermit eleven times, thinking he himself was at fault for his thoughts, he pleaded for helpful guidance. The hermit commented, "Trust me, my son. If God permitted you to experience the imaginings that attack me, you would not be able to resist them. You would be torn apart." His words and deep humility gave the brother relief.

Be careful about your soul.

17 MARCH

Whoever does not carry the cross and follow
me cannot be my disciple. For which of you,
intending to build a tower, does not first sit
down and estimate the cost, to see whether
he has enough to complete it? Otherwise,
when he has laid a foundation and is not
able to finish, all who see it will begin to
ridicule him, saying, "This fellow began to
build and was not able to finish."

LUKE 14:27–30

A HERMIT said, "We fail to make progress because we do not comprehend our capacity. We weary of the work we have started. We want to be good without making any effort."

**Whoever does not carry the cross
and follow me cannot be my disciple.**

18 MARCH

*We gave you this command: Anyone unwilling to work
should not eat.* 2 THESSALONIANS 3:10

JOHN THE DWARF spoke to his elder brother, saying, "I want to be free of responsibilities like the angels. They do no work other than constantly serving God." He then stripped and walked into the desert.

A week later, he returned to his brother. When he knocked on his door, his brother called out "Who's there?"

"It's John."

"John has become an angel and no longer lives with us."

Continuing to pound at the door, he said, "I really am your brother John."

His elder brother refused to open the door, leaving him outdoors until the next morning to teach him a lesson. When he finally opened the door, he said, "If you are a man, you need to work to support yourself. If you are an angel, why do you want to enter my cell?"

Penitent, John said, "Forgive me, my brother."

Anyone unwilling to work should not eat.

A bruised reed he will not break, and a dimly burning wick
he will not quench. ISAIAH 42:3

ABBA ORSISIUS said, "It is my opinion that you must carefully watch your heart. If you do not, you will absent-mindedly become careless with your speech. A lamp produces light when it has oil and a trimmed wick. One may light the wick without a supply of oil, but it will burn away and shadows will gradually come. If a mouse attempts to eat the wick while it is still smoldering, the heat of the dying flame will turn it away. When it knows fire is no longer in the wick, it knocks the lamp to the floor. An earthenware lamp will be shattered, but a brass lamp you may repair.

"If the soul is careless, the Holy Spirit will gradually depart, until it grows cold. Then the enemy chews on the soul, and wickedness breaks it apart. If a good person who truly loves God stumbles into brief carelessness, our merciful God will caution him to watch more carefully in the future."

A dimly burning wick he will not quench.

He who has the bride is the bridegroom.
The friend of the bridegroom, who
stands and hears him, rejoices greatly
at the bridegroom's voice.
For this reason my joy has been fulfilled.
He [Jesus] must increase, but I must decrease.

JOHN 3:29–30

ABBA POEMEN never attempted to say anything superior to what others spoke. He consistently praised their comments.

He must increase, but I must decrease.

21 MARCH

The human spirit will endure sickness. PROVERBS 18:14

AMMA SYNCLETICA said, "When you are sick, do not let it make you miserable, even though you may be too ill to stand for prayer or read a psalm aloud. Such misfortunes are helpful and necessary. They reduce the desires of our body, functioning in the same way as fasting and austerity. If you are ill, you no longer need to fast. As strong medicines cure a disease, so illness itself is a tonic that cures physical passions. You will profit spiritually if you accept illness without complaint, thanking God for it. If we become blind, there is no reason to be upset. We have lost one route to distinction, but now we can contemplate God's glory with the interior eyes of the soul. If we become deaf, then be grateful that small talk will no longer be a distraction. If you have lost the strength of your hands, you will still have the inner strength to resist your enemy's assaults. If disease affects your entire body, you have an opportunity to increase your spiritual health."

If disease affects your body, you have an opportunity to increase in spiritual health.

> *Set a guard over my mouth, O LORD;*
> *keep watch over the door of my lips.*
> PSALM 141:3

A BROTHER had an overwhelming taste for cucumbers. Sometimes he craved them. To control himself, he hung a cucumber from a string in front of him where he could see it all the time. He resisted his desire and did not eat it. He tamed himself, and was sorry that he ever wanted it.

Set a guard over my mouth, O Lord.

Exhort one another every day, as long as it is called "today,"
so that none of you may be hardened by the deceitfulness of sin.
For we have become partners of Christ,
if only we hold our first confidence firm to the end.
HEBREWS 3:13–14

A BROTHER asked Antony to pray for him. Antony answered, "Neither I nor God will have mercy on you until you do something about it yourself. Ask God to help you."

For we are partners of Christ.

I will most gladly spend and be spent for you. If I love you more, am I to be loved less? 2 CORINTHIANS 12:15

TWO BROTHERS took some craft items they had made to town in order to sell them. They separated once they got to town, and one of them had sexual relations with a woman. When the other brother found him at the end of the day and said it was time to return to their cells, the fornicator said he did not want to go.

"Why, brother?"

"Because I succumbed to temptation when you left me. I am guilty of fornication."

Though it was not true, the brother responded, "So did I. After we parted, I was also tempted and fell into fornication. Let's return to our cells and do penance. God will pardon us, sinners that we are."

Arriving at their cells, they reported what they had done and received directions for penance. The innocent brother did not do penance for himself, but for the other, as though he himself had sinned. He laid down his soul for his brother.

I will most gladly spend and be spent.

I have no pleasure in the death of anyone, says the LORD GOD.
Turn, then, and live. EZEKIEL 18:32

ABBA PAUL THE SIMPLE, a disciple of Abba Antony, visited a monastery to help the brethren. After a conversation, the brothers began to gather in the chapel for their customary worship. Paul observed them individually as they entered, noting their degree of piety. As we see faces, Paul could see souls.

As they approached the chapel, Paul observed that while most had a beautiful aura and angels hovered over them, demons darkened one. Temptation led him by the nose, and his angel followed some distance behind, grieving. This moved Paul deeply. He sat down tearfully outside in front of the chapel.

The brothers noticed Blessed Paul's unusual behavior and asked him what was wrong. They were concerned that he might be weeping for all of them. They invited him to join them inside for worship, but he declined. He remained outside, lamenting over the one he had seen.

After worship, as the brothers were exiting, Paul studied them again, wanting to know their spiritual condition. The individual who concerned him had radically changed, with the angel close by and the demons at a distance. Paul jumped with joy and shouted aloud, "Come see what a merciful God can do!"

Everyone gathered around Paul the Simple. He told them what he had seen. The man Paul had singled out came forward and confessed his sin. He said that while he was inside, someone read from Isaiah about scarlet sins becoming white as snow. He accepted it as God's word directly to him and promised that he would renounce sin and serve God with a clean conscience. Everyone rejoiced together.

Turn, then, and live.

*They do all their deeds to be seen by others; for they make
their phylacteries broad and their fringes long.
They love to have the place of honor at banquets and the
best seats in the synagogues, and to be greeted with respect in
the market places, and to have people call them rabbi.*
MATTHEW 23:5–7

AMMA SYNCLETICA said, "Money in an open treasury is soon spent. Any virtue will be lost if it becomes public knowledge. Wax in front of a fire will melt. Shower vain praises on a soul and it will become weak. The soul will look for goodness with less fervor."

**Shower vain praises on a soul
and it will become weak.**

27 MARCH

The bricks have fallen, but we will build with dressed stones;

the sycamores have been cut down,

but we will put cedars in their place.

ISAIAH 9:10

ABBA ALONIUS said, "By utterly destroying myself, I was able to reconstruct and shape myself again in a new way."

**Bricks have fallen,
but we will build with dressed stones.**

Surely, to obey is better than sacrifice,
and to heed than the fat of rams.

1 SAMUEL 15:22

JOHN THE DWARF withdrew into the desert at Scetis to live near an old man of Thebes. His abba planted a stick of dry wood in the sandy soil, instructing John, "Water this every day with a bottle of water until it bears fruit."

Their source of water was far away. John left at sundown and returned at dawn. After three years of this daily routine, the wood lived and bore fruit. The old man carried some of the fruit to church and said to the brothers, "Take and eat the fruit of obedience."

To obey is better than sacrifice.

29 MARCH

Put these things into practice,
devote yourself to them,
so that all may see
your progress.
1 TIMOTHY 4:15

A BROTHER asked Abba Poemen how he should live in his cell. Poemen observed there is a difference between living in one's cell and making progress in the cell. "Living in your cell simply means manual labor, eating once a day, keeping silent, and meditating. Making progress in your cell means you will gain contempt for yourself wherever you go, and that you will not neglect times of secret prayer. If you should have a moment without something to do, fill it with concentrated prayer."

Do not neglect times of secret prayer.

You shall not offer anything that has a blemish,
for it will not be acceptable in your behalf.
LEVITICUS 22:20

A DISCIPLE OF ABBA THEODORE reported to him, "A gardener came today to sell us some onions. He filled a basket with them."

The old man said, "Fill a basket with wheat and give it to him."

The disciple returned and said, "There were two piles of wheat. One was our best wheat and the other was poor. Look, I filled the payment basket with the poor."

Theodore looked at him with anger and sorrow. The disciple prostrated himself before the old man, breaking the basket.

The abba then said, "Get up. It is my fault rather than yours." He then filled his lap with the best wheat and gave it to the gardener who had brought the onions.

You shall not offer anything that has a blemish.

> *Jesus said to him, "Go and do likewise."*
>
> LUKE 10:37

ABBA SISOES asked Abba Or to speak a word for him.

Abba Or asked, "Do you trust me?"

"Yes."

"Go, and do what you have seen me do."

"Abba, what have I seen you do?"

"I think I place myself below all others."

Go and do likewise.

I wore sackcloth;
I afflicted myself with fasting.
I prayed with head bowed on my
bosom, as though
I grieved for a friend
or a brother;
I went about as one
who laments for a mother,
bowed down and in mourning.
PSALM 35:13–14

AMMA SYNCLETICA assured us that in the same way bitter medicine purges illness, prayer and fasting purge us of evil thoughts.

Prayer and fasting purge us.

> *Just as you do not know how the breath*
> *comes to the bones in the mother's womb,*
> *so you do not know the work of God,*
> *who makes everything.*
>
> ECCLESIASTES 11:5

ABBA ANTONY deeply considered God's judgments. He prayed, "Lord, why do some die young while others live to become quite old? Why are some poor and others rich? Why do the wicked prosper and the righteous suffer?" An inner voice answered, "Antony, mind your own business. These things are God's business and none of yours."

These things are God's business.

[Jesus said,] "Keep awake and pray
that you may not
come into the time of trial;
the spirit indeed is willing,
but the flesh is weak."
And again he went away
and prayed.
MARK 14:38–39

B ROTHER JOHN KLIMAKOS said, "When you pray, forget how you may appear to others. Concentrate entirely on your prayer, withdrawing into your heart. Demons fear spiritual concentration more than thieves fear dogs."

Concentrate on your prayer.

When he got up from prayer,
he came to the disciples and found them
sleeping because of grief,
and he said to them,
"Why are you sleeping? Get up and pray
that you may not come into the time of trial."
LUKE 22:45–46

ABBA ARSENIUS would stay awake all night. When overcome with sleep early in the morning he would address it with these words: "Come, impious servant." Then he would doze sitting up. "One hour of sleep is enough for a determined monk."

Get up and pray.

In my distress I called upon the LORD;

to my God I called.

From his temple he heard my voice,

and my cry came to his ears.

2 SAMUEL 22:7

ABBA POEMEN AND ABBA ANOUB were walking in the district of Diolcos. When they passed a cemetery, they saw a grieving woman who was weeping bitterly. They stopped and observed her for a moment. As they continued their walk they met someone and asked, "Why is this woman so grief-stricken?"

"Because she has lost her husband, her son, and her brother."

Abba Poemen commented to Abba Anoub, "Unless we subdue all of our physical desire and grieve like this woman, we cannot be monks. This woman's entire life and soul are distressed."

My cry comes to God's ears.

The tongue is a small member, yet it boasts of great exploits.

JAMES 3:5

A BROTHER approached Abba Poemen during Lent, expressed his thoughts, and found consolation in the response. Then he admitted, "I almost did not come to see you today."

"Why?"

"Since it is Lent, I thought your door might not be opened."

Poemen answered, "We are not taught to shut wooden doors. The door that needs to be closed is the mouth."

The tongue is a small member, yet it boasts of great exploits.

7 APRIL

*I tell you, on the day of judgment you will have to give an
account for every careless word you utter; for by your words you
will be justified, and by your words you will be condemned.*
MATTHEW 12:36–37

ABBA AMMON said, "Meditate as though you were a
criminal in prison. Keep asking, 'Where is my judge?
When will he come? What will be my punishment?' You
should always be awaiting trial. Reproach your soul.
Imagine what it will be like to stand before Christ's
judgment seat and give an account of your behavior. If
you meditate this way, you will be saved."

Always be awaiting trial.

Now we know that the law is good, if one uses it legitimately.
This means understanding that the law is laid down not for the
innocent but for the lawless and disobedient, for the godless and
sinful, for the unholy and profane.

1 TIMOTHY 1:8–9

AN ORDER decreed that religious people in Scetis should fast for a week before the celebration of Easter. During that week, some of the brothers visited Abba Moses in Egypt, who prepared vegetable stew for them. Hermits living in the vicinity observed the smoke and wondered if Moses was disobeying the order by cooking in his cell. The clergy, who respected his extraordinary life, waited until the congregation gathered on Saturday. Then, in front of everyone, they said to him, "Moses, you have broken a human command, but you have observed God's commandments diligently."

The law is good, if one uses it legitimately.

Out of the depths I cry to you, O LORD. Lord, hear my voice!
PSALM 130:1

EVAGRIUS said, "When you are sitting in your cell, think of the day you will die. Admit that your body is decaying. Experience the loss, the pain. Turn away from the vanity of the world. Remain in a quiet place. Ponder the souls in hell. Meditate on their situation— the groaning, the fear, the endless tears. Think of the day of resurrection and God's firm judgment. Imagine the confusion of sinners trembling before God and his Christ, before angels and archangels. See the flames; hear the gnashing of teeth. Then picture the good prepared for the righteous and their confidence before God the father and Christ his son. Keep in mind the treasures of heaven, its joy and peace. Remember all of this. Fear that you may deserve the same condemnation and destruction as other sinners. Desire to enjoy heaven and avoid hell. Never forget these things, whether you are in your cell or outdoors. These mental images will repel dangerous thoughts."

Out of the depths I cry to you, O Lord.

10 APRIL

My eyes will weep bitterly and run down with tears.
JEREMIAH 13:17

ABBA ARSENIUS wore a bib on his chest when he worked. It soaked up the tears that flowed from his eyes.

My eyes will weep bitterly.

Let your ears be attentive to the voice of my supplications!
PSALM 130:2

A N ELDERLY MONK seemed to die, but after several hours, he regained consciousness. A brother asked him, "What did you see, Abba?"

With a serious expression he said, "I heard a sad voice repeating a cry of sorrow. I believe we should lament our sins constantly."

Be attentive to the voice of my supplications.

Be patient, therefore, beloved, until the coming of the Lord.
JAMES 5:7

A BROTHER became tired of his community and the behavior of others often annoyed him. He decided, "I will go off somewhere by myself. Then I will neither talk nor listen and shall be at peace. This anger I feel will depart." He went out into the desert and made his home in a cave.

One day he placed a water jug he had filled on the ground. It rolled over, spilling its contents. He filled it again and it fell over again. When this happened the third time, he became enraged, took hold of the jug and smashed it against the rocks.

Calming down, he realized that anger had mocked him. "Here I am by myself and anger has beaten me. I will return to the community. Wherever we live, we need to work at being patient with God's help."

Work at being patient with God's help.

> *Return, O my soul, to your rest, for the LORD*
> *has dealt bountifully with you.*
> PSALM 116:7

A BROTHER complained to a hermit about his wandering thoughts. The hermit answered, "Keep sitting in your cell and your thoughts will settle down. Hitch a mother donkey to a rail and her foal will dance and prance around, but it always returns to her. The same thing happens for the one who sits patiently in his cell seeking God. His thoughts may wander occasionally, but they will return to God."

Return, O my soul, to your rest.

Let days speak, and many years teach wisdom.
JOB 32:7

THE TEMPTATION to leave his community beset a brother for nine years. Every day he would get ready to go, taking up the cloak he slept in. When night came he thought, "I will leave tomorrow." When the next day dawned, he would think, "I really ought to remain here and resist this temptation for the Lord's sake." He continued this routine every day for nine years. Then the Lord removed the temptation.

Let days speak, and many years teach wisdom.

15 APRIL

Come, let us build ourselves a city, and a tower with its top in
the heavens, and let us make a name for ourselves.

GENESIS 11:4

AMMA SYNCLETICA said, "It is not possible for a seed to be a fully developed tree at the same time. Those who have a reputation in this world cannot bear the fruit of heaven."

It is not possible for a seed
  to be a fully developed tree at the same time.

John [the Baptist] came neither eating nor drinking,
and they say, "He has a demon."

MATTHEW 11:18

A HERMIT said, "If you avoid crowds and turn your back on the world, be prepared to act as though you are the one who is making a mistake."

Act as though you are the one
who is making a mistake.

17 APRIL

Such is the end of all who are greedy for gain;
it takes away the life of its possessors.
PROVERBS 1:19

A BBA AGATHON was taking a journey with some of his followers, one of whom discovered on the road a small bag containing green peas. "Abba, with your permission I will pick it up."

Agathon was incredulous. "Did you put it there?"

"No."

"Then why do you want to pick up something you did not put down?"

Greed takes away the life of its possessors.

The LORD loves those who hate evil; he guards the lives of his faithful; he rescues them from the hand of the wicked.

PSALM 97:10

A HERMIT defined the life of a monk in these ways:
Work
Obedience
Meditation
Avoiding passing judgment
Not speaking evil
Not complaining
Avoiding the wicked
Seeing no evil
Limiting curiosity
Avoiding gossip
Using hands for giving rather than taking
Avoiding pride and bad thoughts
Eating lightly
Making good choices

The Lord guards the lives of his faithful.

The effect of righteousness will be peace, and the result of
righteousness, quietness and trust forever.
ISAIAH 32:17

A HERMIT visited Theodore of Pherme and confessed that he experienced anxiety. Theodore advised him to be humble, putting himself in subjection to others in a religious community. The hermit became a part of a mountain community. Returning to Theodore, he said, "It's no use. I could find no rest even while living with others."

Theodore asked, "If you can't be at peace either as a hermit or as a brother, why did you want to become a monk? You knew that suffering was a part of this life. How long have you been a monk?"

"Eight years."

"Listen to me. I have been a monk for seventy years and I've not had one day of peace yet. Are you looking for peace in only eight years?"

The effect of righteousness will be peace.

The battle is not yours but God's.
2 CHRONICLES 20:15

JOHN THE DWARF asked God to mitigate his passions. He became calm and imperturbable. He told a hermit, "I now rest in peace. There is no struggle between my flesh and my spirit."

The hermit replied, "Pray that the Lord will start a new war in you. Struggle is good for the soul."

When the old conflicts returned John did not pray that God would take them away. Instead, he prayed, "Lord, give me the strength to survive this battle."

Struggle is good for the soul.

I can see that the voyage will be with danger and much heavy loss, not only of the cargo and the ship, but also of our lives.
ACTS 27:10

AMMA SYNCLETICA said, "If you start a good work, do not let the enemy discourage you. Your endurance will defeat the enemy. When sailors encounter unfavorable winds they do not toss their cargo overboard or abandon ship. They struggle against the storm for a while and then reestablish their course. If you run into a headwind, raise a cross as a sail and you will continue your voyage in safety."

Your endurance will defeat the enemy.

Jesus answered them, "Do not complain among yourselves."
JOHN 6:43

A BROTHER reported that when he was in Oxyrhinchus, some of the poor joined them for a Friday evening love feast. Only one of them had a blanket for the night's sleep. He put half of it under him and pulled the other half up on top, but he could not keep warm. The brother said, "When he got up in the middle of the night to relieve himself, I heard him complaining about the cold, but he comforted himself with a prayer."

The poor man said aloud, "Thank you, Lord. Many rich people are in prison tonight, chained and shackled. They are not even able to get up and step outside to relieve themselves. But I am equal to royalty because I can stand and go when I please."

The brother said, "I was near him and I could hear what he said. When I told the brothers, they were enlightened."

Do not complain among yourselves.

23 APRIL

Daniel . . . continued to go to his house, which had windows in its upper room open toward Jerusalem, and to get down on his knees three times a day to pray to his God and praise him, just as he had done previously.

DANIEL 6:10

ABBA NILUS said, "Prayer is the source of gentleness and the manager of anger. It is a remedy for grief and depression."

**Prayer is the source of gentleness
and the manager of anger.**

Not everyone who says to me, "Lord, Lord," will enter
the kingdom of heaven, but only the one who does the
will of my Father in heaven. On that day many will say to me,
"Lord, Lord, did we not prophesy in your name,
and cast out demons in your name, and do many deeds of
power in your name?" Then I will declare to them, "I never
knew you; go away from me, you evildoers."
MATTHEW 7:21–23

THE HERMITS believed that God particularly requires
obedience of anyone recently converted to monastic
life.

**Not everyone who says to me, "Lord, Lord," will
enter the kingdom.**

He was heard because of his reverent submission. Although he
was a Son, he learned obedience through what he suffered.
HEBREWS 5:7–8

A HERMIT expressed his understanding as follows: If you surrender your soul in obedience to a spiritual director, you will have a greater reward than one who merely retreats alone to a hermitage. One of the fathers had a vision of four heavenly ranks.

"The first rank consisted of those who are sick, and still thank God.

"The second was of those who cheerfully take care of the sick.

"The third was of those who live alone in the desert.

"The fourth was of those who, for God's sake, obeyed their spiritual guides. Those in this lowest rank wore glowing necklaces and golden crowns. Why?

"Because those who take care of the sick are doing what they want to do, and hermits make a personal decision to withdraw from the world. But those who obey have gone far beyond their personal choices, depending only on God and the guidance of their spiritual directors. That is why they shine more brightly than the others.

"Obedience is the mother of all virtues. It is the door into God's kingdom. It raises us from earth to heaven. Obedience resides with the angels and is the food of saints."

Obedience is the food of saints.

Since we are receiving a kingdom that cannot be shaken,
let us give thanks, by which we offer to God
an acceptable worship with reverence and awe;
for indeed our God is a consuming fire.
HEBREWS 12:28–29

AMMA SYNCLETICA said, "We will be subjected to great stress and conflict when we begin to follow Christ, but great joy will eventually come. Neophytes are like people trying to light a fire. Smoke gets in their eyes, bringing tears, but they get the job done. We kindle divine fire with tears and difficulties."

We kindle divine fire with tears and difficulties.

Draw me after you, let us make haste.
SONG OF SOLOMON 1:4

MAXIMUS THE CONFESSOR said, "Believe and you will be reverent. Reverence brings humility. Humility makes you gentle. The gentle person controls disorderly desire and aggression, beginning to keep the commandments. Keeping the commandments leads to purity. Purity opens you to inspiration. An inspired person becomes a spouse of the divine Bridegroom and enters his bridal chamber of mysteries."

Draw me after you.

You are the light of the world.
A city built on a hill cannot be hid.
No one after lighting a lamp puts it under the bushel basket,
but on the lampstand, and it gives light to all in the house. In
the same way, let your light shine before others, so that they
may see your good works
and give glory to your Father in heaven.
MATTHEW 5:14–16

THREE FATHERS visited Antony annually. Two would engage in religious discussion, but the third always remained silent. Antony commented, "You often come to see me, but never ask any questions." He replied, "Abba, it is enough to see you."

Let your light shine before others.

Every day I call on you, O LORD;
I spread out my hands to you.
PSALM 88:9

SOME BROTHERS asked Agathon, "Abba, which detail of our way of life is most important?"

Abba Agathon answered, "I could be wrong, but in my opinion prayer to God is the most important and requires all the energy you can give it. When you attempt to pray, demons attempt to interrupt you. They understand that prayer is the only thing that gets in their way. The other aspects of our religious life have a little latitude for rest, but we need to pray to the end of our days. This is the greatest struggle."

We need to pray to the end of our days.

Suppose one of you has a friend, and you go to him at midnight and say to him, "Friend, lend me three loaves of bread; for a friend of mine has arrived, and I have nothing to set before him." And he answers from within, "Do not bother me; the door has already been locked, and my children are with me in bed; I cannot get up and give you anything." I tell you, even though he will not get up and give him anything because he is his friend, at least because of his persistence he will get up and give him whatever he needs.

LUKE 11:5–8

MACARIUS THE GREAT visited Antony on the mountain. When he knocked on his door, Antony came out to meet him, asking his name.

After Macarius identified himself, Antony returned inside, shutting the door behind him. For a long time, Antony could see Macarius waiting patiently at his door.

Finally, he opened the door and welcomed him. "I've heard of you, Macarius. I've wanted to meet you." He showed his visitor every kindness of hospitality. That evening they plaited rope from palm leaves, quietly discussing religion until late at night.

At dawn, Antony went outside to examine the work Macarius had done, as the rope dangled from a window in the cave. He was impressed. Kissing the hand of Macarius, he commented, "There is great virtue in your plaits."

Because of his persistence he will get up and give.

For there is still a vision for the appointed time; it speaks of the end, and does not lie. If it seems to tarry, wait for it; it will surely come, it will not delay.

HABAKKUK 2:3

ABBA ELIAS said, "I fear three things:
This present time before my soul leaves my body.
The time before I see God face to face.
The time before God pronounces my verdict."

There is still a vision for the appointed time.

Now the serpent was more crafty than any other wild animal that the LORD God had made.

GENESIS 3:1

ABBA POEMEN asked Abba Joseph, "What is the best way to deal with temptations? Should I resist them, or let them trouble me?"

Abba Joseph told him, "Let them in and then fight against them."

Poemen returned to his cell in Scetis. One day, a visitor told the brothers he had asked Joseph the same question and was told, "Never let a temptation in. Stop it immediately."

Poemen returned to Joseph at Panephysis and said, "Abba, I entrusted my thoughts to your supervision and you answered me one way while answering a monk from Thebaid the opposite way."

Joseph said, "Do you know that I love you?"

"Yes."

"You wanted me to answer you as though I were speaking for myself. When temptations come, wrestle with them within yourself and they will strengthen you. I told you this as though I were advising myself. Others may not be able to endure this struggle, and it would not be good for them to allow temptations in. They should interrupt them immediately."

**When temptations come,
wrestle with them
and they will strengthen you.**

If you think you are standing, watch out that you do not fall.
No testing has overtaken you that is not common to everyone.
God is faithful, and he will not let you be tested beyond your
strength, but with the testing he will also provide the way out
so that you may be able to endure it.

1 CORINTHIANS 10:12–13

ABBA EVAGRIUS assured us that temptations are an essential part of religious life.

**God will not let you be tested
beyond your strength.**

4 MAY

"Sir, give me this water."

JOHN 4:15

JOHN THE DWARF visited Scetis with some monks. While they were eating, a respected elder offered each of them a drink of water. All of them refused it, except John. This astonished the monks and they asked him later, "How could you, the least of all, accept water from such a distinguished old man?"

John explained, "When I serve water, I like people to take it. That means I've ministered to them. I accepted the water at supper because I wanted the one who served it to have his reward. Perhaps he would have been sorry if no one took any water."

The monks appreciated his judgment.

Sir, give me this water.

5 MAY

He, being compassionate, forgave their
iniquity, and did not destroy them;
often he restrained his anger, and did
not stir up all his wrath. He remembered
that they were but flesh, a wind that passes
and does not come again. How often they rebelled
against him in the wilderness and grieved him in the desert!

PSALM 78:38–40

ABBA ISAAC said, "I never permit any ill feelings against a brother to enter my cell. I have also worked to make sure no brother could return to his cell with any ill feelings toward me."

He, being compassionate, forgave their iniquity.

The LORD is in his holy temple;
let all the earth keep silence before him!
HABAKKUK 2:20

A N EGYPTIAN HERMIT said, "If you desire a spiritual pilgrimage, begin by closing your mouth."

Keep silence before the Lord.

7 MAY

A Canaanite woman from that region came out
and started shouting, "Have mercy on me, Lord,
Son of David; my daughter is tormented by a demon."
But he did not answer her at all. . . . But she came and
knelt before him, saying, "Lord, help me." He answered,
"It is not fair to take the children's food and throw it to the dogs."
She said, "Yes, Lord, yet even the dogs eat the crumbs that fall
from their masters' table." Then Jesus answered her, "Woman,
great is your faith! Let it be done for you as you wish."
And her daughter was healed instantly.

MATTHEW 15:22–28

ABBA POEMEN said, "I will explain why we must struggle so desperately. It is because we do not love others as the Scripture teaches. We also forget the Canaanite woman who followed the Lord, pleading with him to cure her daughter."

Have mercy on me, Lord.

> *Hear, my child, and accept my words,*
> *that the years of your life may be many.*
> PROVERBS 4:10

ABBA SISOES pondered the question, "Why did you leave Scetis, where you lived with Abba Or, and withdraw to live here?"

The old man answered, "Scetis became crowded. I learned that Antony had died, so I got up and came here to this mountain. Discovering the peaceful nature of this place, I settled here for a little while."

"How long have you been here?"

"Seventy-two years."

Accept my words
that the years of your life may be many.

9 *MAY

Who will separate us from
the love of Christ?
Will hardship,
or distress, or persecution,
or famine, or nakedness,
or peril, or sword?

ROMANS 8:35

WHILE ABBA DANIEL AND ABBA AMMOES were traveling together, Abba Ammoes asked, "When will we settle down in a cell like others?"

Abba Daniel said, "Who can separate us from God? God is in the cell, but God is also outdoors."

Who can separate us from God?

Do not love the world or the things in the world. The love of the Father is not in those who love the world; for all that is in the world—the desire of the flesh, the desire of the eyes, the pride in riches—comes not from the Father but from the world.

1 JOHN 2:15–16

A MONK informed Abba Theodore that a brother had returned to the world. Theodore responded, "Don't let that surprise you. The surprising thing is when you learn that someone has successfully escaped the jaws of the enemy."

Do not love the things in the world.

The sayings of the wise are like goads, and like nails firmly fixed are the collected sayings that are given by one shepherd. Of anything beyond these, my child, beware. Of making many books there is no end, and much study is a weariness of the flesh.

ECCLESIASTES 12:11–12

A HERMIT said, "The prophets wrote books. Another generation followed them and studied those books assiduously, memorizing them. Our generation carefully copies them onto papyrus and parchment, but we leave them unread on the windowsill."

The sayings of the wise are like goads.

In everything do to others as you would have them do to you;
for this is the law and the prophets.

MATTHEW 7:12

HYPERICHIUS taught, "As much as possible, guide your neighbor away from sin, but do not condemn him. God does not refuse any seeking person. Never allow an unkind comment regarding your brother to linger in your mind. Always be prepared to say, 'Forgive us our trespasses, as we forgive those who trespass against us.'"

Always be prepared to say,
"Forgive us our trespasses."

Jesus, looking at him, loved him and said,
  "You lack one thing; go, sell what you own,
  and give the money to the poor,
  and you will have treasure in heaven;
    then come, follow me."

MARK 10:21

EVAGRIUS PONTICUS wrote, "The only thing owned by one of our brothers was a book of the Gospels. He sold it and gave the proceeds for the support of the poor. What he said is worth remembering. 'I have sold the book that tells me to sell my possessions and give the money to the poor.'"

Seek heavenly treasure.

14 MAY

Be steadfast, immovable,
always excelling in the
work of the Lord,
because you know
that in the Lord your labor
is not in vain.

1 CORINTHIANS 15:58

ABBA AGATHON said, "I consider no other labor as difficult as prayer. When we are ready to pray, our spiritual enemies interfere. They understand it is only by making it difficult for us to pray that they can harm us. Other things will meet with success if we keep at it, but laboring at prayer is a war that will continue until we die."

Your labor is not in vain.

When Simon Peter saw
[that the boats were full of fish],
he fell down at Jesus' knees, saying,
"Go away from me, Lord,
for I am a sinful man!"
LUKE 5:8

AN OLDER MONK AND A YOUNGER MONK were in Cellia. The older suggested that they live together. The younger refused, saying, "I am a sinner, Abba. I must not live with you." But the older monk insisted. The old man was pure in heart, and the younger monk did not want him to discover that he sometimes had sexual cravings.

The older monk said, "I will go away for a week. When I return, we can talk about this again."

Seven days later, the younger decided to test the older by saying, "While you were gone, I was strongly tempted. I went into town on an errand, and I ended up in bed with a woman."

The older monk asked, "Are you penitent?"

"Yes."

"Then I will carry half the burden of this sin with you."

The younger man responded, "Now I know we can stay together."

They remained companions until death separated them.

I will carry half the burden of this sin with you.

Is not my word like fire, says the LORD, and like a
hammer that breaks a rock in pieces?
JEREMIAH 23:29

JOHN, whom Emperor Marcion had exiled, reported that he and others went to Syria to visit Abba Poemen. They had questions about hardness of heart, but Poemen did not understand the Greek they spoke. No one could interpret for them, and Poemen observed their embarrassment. Speaking in Greek, Poemen said, "Water is naturally soft and stone is naturally hard. But let water drip continuously on a stone and it will erode. The word of God works the same way. It is soft and our hearts are hard, but if we hear the word of God frequently, it will open our hearts to reverence."

**If we hear the word of God frequently,
it will open our hearts to reverence.**

17 MAY

Even now the ax is lying at the root of the trees; every tree therefore that does not bear good fruit is cut down and thrown into the fire.

MATTHEW 3:10

SOMEONE asked Abba Agathon whether physical or spiritual discipline was the most difficult. He said, "We are like trees. The leaves are similar to bodily discipline, and the fruit is like spiritual discipline. We need to be careful about guarding the thoughts of our mind, because they are our fruit. At the same time, attractive leaves should cover us, which is physical discipline. It is important to do manual labor, and to be careful about our food and clothing."

Be careful to guard the thoughts of our mind; they are our fruit.

The LORD has punished me severely,
but he did not give me over to death.

PSALM 118:18

AMMA SYNCLETICA said, "The devil uses both poverty and wealth to tempt us. When ridicule and derision do not succeed, he uses praise and flattery. If he does not conquer through good health, he tries illness. If ease does not lead us astray, he calls upon aggravations that tempt us to renounce our monastic vows. The devil inflicts severe illness on those he wants to force away from God. When this happens, endure it. Remember you are a sinner and another world is waiting for you. Fire cleanses iron of rust. When the righteous suffer, they move to a higher sanctity. If you receive a thorn in the flesh, thank God that you have received a gift like Paul's. If you experience chills and fevers, recall this text of Scripture, 'We went through fire and through water; yet you have brought us out to a spacious place' (Psalm 66:12). Allow every difficulty to test our souls, because the enemy is always nearby."

You have brought us out to a spacious place.

19 MAY

Then Jesus told them a parable
about their need to pray always
and not to lose heart.
LUKE 18:1

EVAGRIUS PONTICUS wrote, "Prayer is a constant exchange of the human spirit with God. Consider the special condition of soul that is necessary for the spirit to reach out unhesitatingly to its Master, living in God's presence with no assistance from anyone else."

Prayer is a constant exchange
of the human spirit with God.

By his great mercy he has given us a new birth into a living hope through the resurrection of Jesus Christ from the dead, and into an inheritance that is imperishable, undefiled, and unfading, kept in heaven for you.

1 PETER 1:3–4

AN ADMINISTRATOR delivered a last will and testament to Abba Arsenius. A relative who was a senator had left Arsenius a large bequest. Arsenius took the document in his hands, preparing to rip it to shreds. The administrator fell at his feet, saying, "Please do not destroy it. I will be blamed."

Arsenius said, "I died first. How can he now make me his heir?" He returned the will, accepting nothing.

Our true inheritance is Christ.

See that none of you repays evil for evil,
but always seek to do good
to one another and to all.
1 THESSALONIANS 5:15

A BROTHER asked Abba Poemen to comment on the text, "Do not repay evil for evil." Abba Poemen replied, "Emotions function in four stages: first in the heart, second in facial expression, third in speech, and fourth in action. If your heart is pure, your face will show it. If your facial expression reveals your rising passion, avoid saying anything about it. If words come from your mouth, stop speaking as quickly as you can. Otherwise, you may repay evil for evil."

Do not repay evil for evil.

God is our refuge and strength,
a very present help in trouble.
　　PSALM 46:1

ABBA MOSES said, "If your behavior does not match your prayers, your prayers are wasted. We should not continue to do anything we condemn in our prayers. If we surrender our personal will, God will accept our prayers."

God is our refuge and strength.

> *If anyone wants to sue you and take your coat,*
> *give your cloak as well; and if anyone*
> *forces you to go one mile, go also the*
> *second mile. Give to everyone who begs*
> *from you, and do not refuse anyone*
> *who wants to borrow from you.*
> MATTHEW 5:40–42

AN UNIDENTIFIED ABBA said, "If you are asked for something, even if it is an order backed by force, let your heart go with the gift. When you give something away, give it with a willing heart."

Give with a willing heart.

*The LORD God took the man and put him in
the garden to till it and keep it.*

GENESIS 2:15

SOME MONKS, well known as men of prayer, visited Abba Lucius, who asked them if they did any manual labor. They replied, "We don't do any work with our hands. We obey St. Paul's instruction to pray without ceasing."

Lucius asked them if they ate.

"Yes, of course we do."

"When you eat, who prays for you? Do you sleep?"

"Yes."

"When you are asleep, who prays for you?"

They had no answer for him.

"Perhaps I am wrong, brothers, but it appears to me that you do not do what you say you do. I pray without ceasing, but I also work with my hands. I will describe my technique for you. Asking God to help me, I sit down with some palm leaves, 'Have mercy on me, O God, according to your steadfast love; according to your abundant mercy blot out my transgressions (Psalm 51:1).' Do you think that is a prayer?"

"It certainly is a prayer."

"When I pray in my heart all day while I am working, I make a little money. I put some of it outside my door and buy food with the remainder. Whoever finds the coins outside my door prays for me while I am eating and sleeping. This is how I keep St. Paul's injunction."

God put him in the garden to till it and keep it.

2 5 MAY

Set your minds on things that are above, not on things that are
on earth, for you have died, and your life is hidden with Christ
in God. When Christ who is your life is revealed, then you also
will be revealed with him in glory.

COLOSSIANS 3:2–4

DURING A CONVERSATION between two desert hermits,
one said, "I am dead to the world."

The other responded, "You should not be so sure of that until you actually die. You may think that you are dead to the world, but Satan is still alive."

**You have died, and your life is hidden
with Christ in God.**

I pray that, according to the riches of his glory, he may grant
that you may be strengthened in your inner being with power
through his Spirit, and that Christ may dwell in your hearts
through faith, as you are being rooted and grounded in love.
EPHESIANS 3:16–17

A DESERT HERMIT said, "You are like a house, and the devil is like an antagonistic neighbor. The enemy throws a lot of dirty garbage into your house. It is your job to clean out whatever he throws in. If you fail to do this, your house will fill with so much corruption you will not be able to enter. The moment he begins to shovel dirt, clean it out, little by little. With Christ's help, you can keep a tidy house."

You are being rooted and grounded in love.

27 MAY

When the Lamb opened the seventh seal,

there was silence in heaven

for about half an hour.

REVELATION 8:1

A HERMIT said, "Remember to keep silent. Empty your mind. Concentrate on your meditation with reverence for God, whether you are resting or working. If you will do this, you have no need to worry about attacks from demons."

**Concentrate on your meditation
with reverence for God.**

*Moses said, "I must turn aside and look at this great sight, and
see why the bush is not burned up." When the LORD saw that
he had turned aside to see, God called to him out of the bush,
"Moses, Moses!" And he said, "Here I am." Then he said,
"Come no closer! Remove the sandals from your feet."*
EXODUS 3:3–5

EVAGRIUS PONTICUS wrote, "When Moses wanted to
get closer to the burning bush, he was not allowed
to do so until he took off his shoes. In the same way, if
we desire to see the One who is beyond our thought and
perception, we must be free of every thought tainted with
passion."

Be free of every thought tainted with passion.

He will command his angels concerning you

to guard you in all your ways.

On their hands they will bear you up,

so that you will not dash your foot against a stone.

PSALM 91:11–12

BROTHER JOHN KLIMAKOS said, "If you feel a special joy when you are praying, or experience a movement inside yourself, continue in your prayers. Your guardian angel has come and is praying with you."

His angels will bear you up.

How often is the lamp of the wicked put out? How often does calamity come upon them? How often does God distribute pains in his anger? How often are they like straw before the wind, and like chaff that the storm carries away?

JOB 21:17–18

A BROTHER commented to a hermit, "Nothing disturbs my soul."

The hermit replied, "You have a wide open door. Anyone may enter and exit without attracting your attention. If you would shut and lock the door, wicked thoughts could not enter. Then you could see them standing outside, trying to get in."

Shut and lock the door against wicked thoughts.

Lament and mourn and weep.
Let your laughter be turned into mourning
and your joy into dejection.
Humble yourselves before the Lord, and he will exalt you.
JAMES 4:9–10

EVAGRIUS PONTICUS wrote, "Let your first prayer be for the gift of tears. Sorrow will soften your natural disrespect. Once you have confessed your sins to the Lord, he will forgive you. When you pray with tears, God will pay close attention. Nothing pleases the Lord more than an entreaty accompanied by tears.

"Though fountains of tears flow during your prayer, never think that you are better than others. Your prayers have simply received the help you need to confess your sins without hindrance."

When you pray with tears,
God will pay close attention.

We know that our old self was crucified with him so that the
body of sin might be destroyed,
and we might no longer be enslaved to sin.
ROMANS 6:6

A HERMIT said, "A monk should examine himself morning and evening, every day, asking himself how well he has conformed to the will of God. Each new day is an opportunity for penance. Abba Arsenius lived that way."

Our old self was crucified with him.

2 JUNE

If they were wise, they would understand this;
they would discern what the end would be.

DEUTERONOMY 32:29

* * * * *

As a HERMIT lay on his deathbed in Scetis, the brothers stood around him, weeping. But three times the dying man opened his eyes and laughed. One of the brothers asked him, "Abba, why do you laugh when we are crying?"

He answered, "I laughed the first time because you are afraid of dying. I laughed the second time because you are not prepared to die. I laughed the third time because I am moving from labor to rest, and yet you weep." Then he closed his eyes and died.

I am moving from labor to rest, and yet you weep.

3 JUNE

Ask, and it will be given you; search, and you will find; knock,
and the door will be opened for you. For everyone who asks
receives, and everyone who searches finds, and for everyone who
knocks, the door will be opened.
MATTHEW 7:7–8

ABBA ANTONY met Abba Amoun at Mount Nitria. Abba Amoun said, "Your prayers have resulted in increased participation here. Some of the brothers want to build cells where they can be at peace. How far away do you think they should go?" Abba Antony suggested they eat at the ninth hour and then explore the desert. They walked until sunset, when Antony said, "Let's pray and erect a cross here. Anyone who wishes may build a cell here. That way, visitors can eat a little food at the ninth hour and walk here without distraction." Twelve miles separated the sites.

Ask, seek, knock.

4 JUNE

The LORD said to Moses: Take sweet spices,
stacte, and onycha, and galbanum, sweet spices
with pure frankincense (an equal part of each),
and make an incense blended as by the perfumer,
seasoned with salt, pure and holy.

EXODUS 30:34–35

EVAGRIUS PONTICUS wrote, "If you want to make a fragrant perfume, you must mix pure incense with cinnamon, onyx, and myrrh in equal parts as directed in the law. This mixture represents the four great moral virtues. To be faithful to the spirit, they must be present in full strength and correct proportions. When your soul is purified in this way, it will be healthy and well-balanced."

Make an incense,
seasoned with salt, pure and holy.

5 JUNE

Love is patient; love is kind; love is not envious
or boastful or arrogant or rude.
1 CORINTHIANS 13:4–5

A BROTHER visited Theodore of Pherme for three days, seeking his guidance. Theodore never said anything to him, and he departed disheartened.

Theodore's disciple asked, "Abba, why did you refuse to speak with him? He was sad when he left us."

Theodore replied, "I'll tell you why I did not talk with him. He wasn't interested in what I had to say. He only wanted to receive credit by telling others what he heard me say."

Love is not envious or boastful.

What good is it, my brothers and sisters, if you say you have faith but do not have works? Can faith save you? If a brother or sister is naked and lacks daily food, and one of you says to them, "Go in peace; keep warm and eat your fill," and yet you do not supply their bodily needs, what is the good of that? So faith by itself, if it has no works, is dead.

JAMES 2:14–17

A HERMIT said, "Idle talking is wasted time. There is plenty of chattering going on today, but what we need is action. God prefers the application of faith instead of pointless conversation."

Faith, if it has no works, is dead.

7 JUNE

*The beginning of wisdom is this: Get wisdom, and whatever
else you get, get insight. Prize her highly, and she will exalt
you; she will honor you if you embrace her.*

PROVERBS 4:7–8

D IADOCHOS OF PHOTIKE said, "All gifts of God are
beautiful beyond description and are the source of
all our righteousness. The one that can inflame our souls
and motivate us to love goodness itself is the gift of divine
understanding. This is the starting point for all of God's
wonderful gifts to the soul. It severs our relationship with
obsessive desire for corruptible things, and opens the way
to increasing love for the riches of divine comprehension.
Once we receive it, we burn with an uplifting flame and
join the celebration of angels."

God's first gift is divine understanding.

8 JUNE

From new moon to new moon, and from Sabbath to Sabbath,
all flesh shall come to worship before me, says the LORD.

ISAIAH 66:23

TWO DESERT HERMITS met and cooked some lentils. They decided to worship God before they ate. One of them recited all of the psalms; the other read and meditated upon two Major Prophets. When morning came, the visiting hermit departed. They never ate their lentils.

All flesh shall come to worship
before me, says the Lord.

9 JUNE

How long will you torment me,
and break me in pieces with words?
JOB 19:2

EVAGRIUS PONTICUS wrote, "Focus your attention on your prayer. Do not allow any other thoughts to distract you. All they will do is interrupt your prayer. When the devils understand that you are serious about fervent prayer, they will suggest subtle things that seem important. Soon enough, you will be unable to continue praying. This will discourage you."

Focus your attention on your prayer.

10 JUNE

Seven times a day I praise you for your righteous ordinances.
Great peace have those who love your law;
nothing can make them stumble.

PSALM 119:164–165

ABBA EPIPHANIUS reminded us that David prayed late at night, in the middle of the night, and before dawn. He stood before God in the wee hours of darkness. In the evening and at noon he continued to pray. He said in his psalm, "I praise you seven times a day."

Those who love God's law have great peace.

> *Consider and answer me, O LORD my God!*
> *Give light to my eyes,*
> *or I will sleep the sleep of death,*
> *and my enemy will say,*
> *"I have prevailed."*
> PSALM 13:3–4

A HERMIT said, "Cover a donkey's eyes and it will walk in circles around the mill wheel. If you uncover its eyes, it will not continue to walk. The devil obscures our vision and leads us into all kinds of sins. If we keep our eyes open, we will more likely escape."

Answer me, O Lord my God!
Give light to my eyes.

Let the words of my mouth and the meditation of my heart be acceptable to you, O LORD, my rock and my redeemer.

PSALM 19:14

ABBA POEMEN said, "If someone does not speak, but looks down on other people, he is actually talking continuously. Someone else may talk all day, but is keeping silence if he always speaks in a holy manner."

**Let the words of my mouth
and the meditation of my heart be acceptable.**

> *When you are praying, do not heap up empty phrases as*
> *the Gentiles do; for they think that they will be heard*
> *because of their many words. Do not be like them, for*
> *your Father knows what you need before you ask him.*
> MATTHEW 6:7–8

WHEN SOME BROTHERS asked Abba Macarius how to pray, he said, "Prayer does not require a lot of language. Frequently reach out your hands, saying, 'Lord, have mercy on me. I trust you.' If some struggle worries you, simply say, 'Lord, help me.' God knows what is best for us, and God is merciful."

When you are praying,
do not heap up empty phrases.

Woe is me! I am lost,
for I am a man of unclean lips,
and I live among a people of unclean lips;
yet my eyes have seen the King,
the LORD of hosts!"
ISAIAH 6:5

EVAGRIUS PONTICUS wrote, "If you think you do not need to accompany your prayers with tears for your sins, consider the great distance that separates you from God. Understand that we are designed to be near God all the time. Then your tears will flow freely."

You should be near God all the time.

> *Then Peter began to speak to them:*
>> *"I truly understand that God shows no partiality,*
>> *but in every nation anyone who fears him and*
>> *does what is right is acceptable to him."*
>> ACTS 10:34

WHEN ARSENIUS asked an elderly Egyptian monk some questions, another person commented, "Abba Arsenius, you have a strong education in Latin and Greek. Why do you discuss anything with this peasant?" He replied, "True. I have knowledge of Latin and Greek, but I do not yet know this man's alphabet."

God shows no partiality.

Whoever is slow to anger has great understanding,
but one who has a hasty temper exalts folly.
A tranquil mind gives life to the flesh,
but passion makes the bones rot.

PROVERBS 14:29–30

MACARIUS said, "If you become angry when you are admonishing someone, you are satisfying your own passions. Do not lose yourself while attempting to save someone else."

A tranquil mind gives life to the flesh.

Beware of the scribes,
who like to walk around in long robes,
and love to be greeted with respect in the marketplaces,
and to have the best seats in the synagogues
and places of honor at banquets.
LUKE 20:46

WHILE THE COMMUNITY considered Antony a person filled with the Holy Spirit, he never talked about his relationship with God.

Disdain the seat of honor.

Do you not know that in a race the runners all compete,
but only one receives the prize?
Run in such a way that you may win it.
1 CORINTHIANS 9:24

SOMEONE asked a hermit how he could avoid being shocked when he saw monks returning to the world. He said, "Think of hounds chasing a rabbit. One dog sees the rabbit and begins the chase, the rest of the pack simply see and hear a hound running. They will join the lead dog for a while, but soon tire and return the way they came. Only the first hound continues the chase until he overtakes the rabbit. The desertion of his companions does not discourage him. Thickets, briars, and cliffs will not turn him aside. Scratched and wounded, he continues to chase the rabbit. So it is with anyone who runs after the Lord Jesus. We keep our eyes on the cross, leaping over every obstacle until we come to him."

Run in such a way that you may win.

Alas for those who are at ease in Zion,
and for those who feel secure on Mount Samaria.
AMOS 6:1

* * * * * * *

A HERMIT said, "Satan has three powers that lead us into all sins:

Forgetfulness,

Negligence,

Selfish desire.

If forgetfulness comes, the result is negligence, and negligence is the source of selfish desire. Selfish desire will be our downfall. A serious mind will not be forgetful, and negligence will not become a problem. With Christ's help, selfish desire will not rule us."

With Christ's help, selfish desire will not rule us.

Sing to him, sing praises to him;
tell of all his wonderful works.
Glory in his holy name;
let the hearts of those who seek the LORD rejoice.
Seek the LORD and his strength;
seek his presence continually.

PSALM 105:2–4

EVAGRIUS said, "If you have not yet received the grace of prayer or psalmody, keep trying with enthusiasm. You will gain it."

Seek the Lord and his strength.

I turned to the LORD God, to seek an answer by prayer and
supplication with fasting and sackcloth and ashes.
DANIEL 9:3

EULOGIUS, a priest and student of John the bishop, would fast for two days and sometimes an entire week, nibbling a little bread and salt. He was highly regarded. Desiring greater asceticism, Eulogius visited Abba Joseph at Panephysis. The old man welcomed him and offered everything he could to refresh him. Those who came with Eulogius explained, "All the priest eats is bread and salt." Abba Joseph ate without comment.

The visitors remained three days, but never heard any chanting or prayers. Their host's entire group engaged in private spiritual discipline. The guests learned nothing.

On their way home, Eulogius and his disciples lost their way in the night and decided to return to Panephysis. As they approached the door, they could hear chanting inside. After waiting for a pause in the singing, they knocked on the door. Again, they were welcomed warmly.

Because of the heat, the companions of Eulogius hurried to the water jar and offered him a drink. Because it was a mixture of sea and river water, it was not palatable.

Eulogius knelt before the old man and asked, "Abba, explain to us why you did not chant while we were with you, but only when we departed. And why is there salt water in your jug?" At first, the old man denied it, suggesting that they had mistakenly mixed seawater with it. Eulogius insisted they had not, and begged the old man for the truth.

"We keep this little bottle of wine for our visitors, but that water is what we drink." He went on to instruct Eulogius about discernment of thoughts and self-control, saying that he ate whatever anyone brought to him and was spiritually active in secret.

Eulogius commented, "Your way of life is certainly genuine."

Enter your closet to pray.

If any of you put a stumbling block
before one of these little ones who believe in me,
it would be better for you
if a great millstone were hung around your neck
and you were thrown into the sea.

MARK 9:42

A MOUN found Abba Poemen and told him, "When I visit a neighbor or he visits me, we hesitate to talk with each other. We are afraid that we might bring up a secular topic."

The old man replied, "Yes, young people need to guard their mouths."

Amoun asked, "But how do old men handle this problem?"

Abba Poemen said, "Those who have advanced in virtue no longer have any worldliness in them. Nothing will taint their speech."

Amoun continued his questioning. "When I must speak with my neighbor, should I speak of the Scriptures or of the Fathers?"

The old man answered, "It is best to keep silence. If you can't, talk about the sayings of the Fathers. Speaking about the Scriptures is risky."

Guard your conversation.

To all who received him, who believed in his name,
he gave power to become children of God,
who were born, not of blood or of the will of the flesh
or of the will of man, but of God.
JOHN 1:12–13

THE THOUGHT often occurred to a hermit to rest today and do penance tomorrow. He would challenge his thought by saying, "No! I will do penance today. May God's will be done tomorrow."

To all who believed in his name,
he gave power to become children of God.

24 JUNE

Athletes exercise self-control in all things; they do it to receive a
perishable wreath, but we an imperishable one.

1 CORINTHIANS 9:25

AMMA SYNCLETICA said, "Worldly pleasures and treasures should not attract you as something worthwhile to have. We respect the art of cooking because it brings pleasure to the palate. You may fast rigorously to subdue that pleasure. Don't keep enough bread to satisfy your hunger, and control your thirst for wine."

Exercise self-control in all things.

Out of the heart come evil intentions,
murder, adultery, fornication, theft,
false witness, slander.
These are what defile a person.
MATTHEW 15:19–20

A BROTHER asked some monks, "Do evil thoughts defile us?"

They answered with divided opinions. Some thought they do us harm, but others said, "Not at all. If they did, none of us has a chance. There is a difference between thinking evil and doing evil."

The brother was not satisfied with their conflicting answers. He found a knowledgeable hermit and asked him the same question. The hermit replied, "All of us are required to act the best we are able."

"Please, for the Lord's sake, explain what you mean."

"Suppose I had a valuable jug that two monks see. One of the monks has more ability for a disciplined life than the other. If the stronger monk is attracted to the jug, but immediately rejects the thought of taking it, the thought does not defile him. On the other hand, if the weaker monk covets the jug and considers stealing it, but then after an inner struggle resists the temptation, then neither is he defiled."

All of us are required to act the best we are able.

26 JUNE

Aspire to live quietly,
to mind your own affairs,
and to work with your hands.
1 THESSALONIANS 4:11

AMMA MACRINA lived a liberated life, like the freedom of a soul released by death. She lived apart from the trivial things of the world, in harmony with angels.

Aspire to live quietly,
and to work with your hands.

Yours is the day, yours also the night;
you established the luminaries and the sun.
You have fixed all the bounds of the earth;
you made summer and winter.
PSALM 74:16–17

A BROTHER asked a hermit, "If I oversleep and miss the time for prayer, I hesitate to keep the rule of prayer. I am embarrassed and do not want the brothers to hear me praying."

The hermit gave him this advice: "If you sleep late, get up and shut your door and windows. Then pray your psalms. Both day and night belong to God. You will glorify God whatever time it is."

Both day and night belong to God.

O that I had wings like a dove!
I would fly away and be at rest;
truly, I would flee far away;
I would lodge in the wilderness;
I would hurry to find a shelter for myself
from the raging wind and tempest.
PSALM 55:6–8

ABBA ARSENIUS stood by some reeds rustling in the wind. "The song of a little sparrow can destroy the peace of one who is living in silent prayer. The noise of these reeds is much worse."

O that I had wings like a dove!

29 JUNE

Return to me, says the LORD of hosts,
and I will return to you.

ZECHARIAH 1:3

A HERMIT pointed out that a person near the emperor is safe from harm. "Satan cannot harm us if we stay near God. It is because we frequently become victims of pride that it is easy for the enemy to lead our miserable souls into physical passion and humiliation."

Return to me, says the Lord of hosts.

Be appalled, O heavens, at this,
be shocked, be utterly desolate,
says the LORD, for my people have committed two evils:
they have forsaken me, the fountain of living water,
and dug out cisterns for themselves,
cracked cisterns that can hold no water.
JEREMIAH 2:12–13

THE HERMITS had a saying, "If you see a young person climbing up to heaven by his own strength, catch him by the foot and drag him back down to earth. It is not good for him."

God is the fountain of living water.

Put away from you all bitterness and wrath and anger
and wrangling and slander, together with all malice,
and be kind to one another, tenderhearted,
forgiving one another, as God in Christ has forgiven you.
EPHESIANS 4:31–32

S OME BROTHERS asked Abba Silvanus to tell them the secret of his remarkable discretion.

Silvanus replied, "I never allow any bitter thought to remain in my heart."

Put away from you all
bitterness and wrath and anger.

I said, "I will guard my ways that I may not sin with my tongue; I will keep a muzzle on my mouth."
PSALM 39:1

ABBA PETER asked Abba Agathon the secret of living with other monks. He said, "Always remain a stranger. Familiarity is like a strong wind that sweeps away everything before it, destroying the fruit of the trees." Peter wanted to know if social conversation was that negative. Agathon replied, "An uncontrolled tongue is the worst of all passions. It is the mother of all other passions."

**I will guard my ways that
I may not sin with my tongue.**

> *Do not store up for yourselves treasures on earth,*
> *where moth and rust consume and where thieves break in*
> *and steal; but store up for yourselves treasures in heaven,*
> *where neither moth nor rust consumes and where*
> *thieves do not break in and steal.*
> MATTHEW 6:19–20

AMMA SYNCLETICA said, "Live a sober life. Destructive thieves enter through our physical senses. The smoke that is stifling outside will blacken the walls of our house if it finds an easy way in through open windows."

Store up for yourselves treasures in heaven.

The LORD sits enthroned over the flood;
the LORD sits enthroned as king forever.
May the LORD give strength to his people!
May the LORD bless his people with peace!
PSALM 29:10–11

ABBA SERAPION said, "Imperial guards serving duty in the emperor's presence keep their eyes straight ahead and do not turn their heads. The monk in God's presence must focus all of his attention on reverence. If he will do this, none of the enemy's advances will threaten him."

May the Lord give strength to his people!

5 JULY

You have heard that it was said to those of ancient times,
"You shall not murder"; and "whoever murders shall be liable
to judgment." But I say to you that if you are angry with a
brother or sister, you will be liable to judgment.

MATTHEW 5:21–22

ABBA AGATHON said, "If someone who is angry were
to raise the dead, God would remain displeased with
the anger."

Anger always displeases God.

When Jesus saw the crowds,
he went up the mountain;
and after he sat down,
his disciples came to him.
Then he began to speak,
and taught them.
MATTHEW 5:1–2

ABBA EVAGRIUS said, "Restrain your desire to mingle socially. Crowds of people distract your spirit and disturb inner peace." Abba Doulas expressed the idea this way: "Detach yourself from the enjoyment of crowds or your enemy will challenge your spirit and disturb your inner peace."

Crowds of people distract
your spirit and disturb inner peace.

7 JULY

Abraham, having patiently endured, obtained the promise.
HEBREWS 6:15

ABBA POEMEN said, "Put a snake or scorpion in a box and it will eventually die. Evil thoughts planted by the demons will gradually lose their influence if you resist them long enough."

**Abraham patiently endured
and obtained the promise.**

> *[Jesus said,]*
> *"If I had not come and spoken to them,*
> *they would not have sin;*
> *but now they have no excuse*
> *for their sin."*
> JOHN 15:22

ABBA ANTONY told Abba Poemen, "We have one great work to accomplish. Before God, we must accept responsibility for our sins, expecting to be tempted until our last breath."

We must accept responsibility for our sins.

Where is the debater of this age?
Has not God made foolish the wisdom of the world?
For since, in the wisdom of God, the world did not know
God through wisdom, God decided,
through the foolishness of our proclamation,
to save those who believe.

1 CORINTHIANS 1:20–21

SOME QUARRELING PEOPLE asked Abba Ammon to decide their case for them. Ammon paid no attention to them. He then overheard a woman remark, "This hermit is an old fool."

Ammon called her to himself and said, "You will never know how hard I have worked in the desert to be considered a fool. Now you have noticed that I am naturally foolish. Thank you for showing me that all my attempts to imitate folly were unnecessary."

God has made foolish the wisdom of the world.

Who set wild donkeys free?
I alone help them survive in salty desert sand.
They stay far from crowded cities and refuse to be tamed.
Instead, they roam the hills, searching for pastureland.
JOB 39:5–8 CEV

ABBA ISAIAH said that a beginner who moves from one monastery to another is like an animal desperately trying to avoid the halter.

Who set wild donkeys free?

If anyone strikes you on the right cheek, turn the other also.

MATTHEW 5:39

ABBA DANIEL reported that a Babylonian nobleman's daughter was demon possessed. Her father asked a monk to help her. The monk replied, "The only ones who can help your daughter are some hermits I know. The problem is, their humility will prompt them to decline your request for assistance. Let's try this: when they bring their produce to town for sale, tell them you want to buy it. When they come to your home for payment, we will ask for their prayers. I think your daughter will be cured."

Going out into the street, they found a disciple of a hermit who was sitting there selling baskets. He accompanied them home for his payment. As the monk entered the house, the possessed girl approached him and slapped his face. The monk did what his Lord commanded, turning his other cheek to her.

This dislodged the demon from her and it began to cry out, "Violence! The commandment of Jesus Christ is destroying me!" Healing came to the girl.

Returning to the hermit, they reported what had happened. He gave God the glory, saying, "Even the pride of demons falls before humble obedience to the commandments of Jesus Christ."

**If anyone strikes you on the right cheek,
turn the other also.**

Two men went up to the temple to pray, one a Pharisee and the other a tax collector. The Pharisee, standing by himself, was praying thus, "God, I thank you that I am not like other people: thieves, rogues, adulterers, or even like this tax collector. I fast twice a week; I give a tenth of all my income." But the tax collector, standing far off, would not even look up to heaven, but was beating his breast and saying, "God, be merciful to me, a sinner!"

LUKE 18:10–13

ABBA HYPERICHIUS said, "The tree of life is tall. Only humility can climb it. Be like the tax collector if you do not want to be condemned with the Pharisee. Follow gentle Moses and chip out the rocky places of your heart that they may become springs of water."

God, be merciful to me, a sinner!

> *Let anyone who has an ear*
>> *listen to what the Spirit is saying to the churches.*
>>> *To everyone who conquers*
>>> *I will give some of the hidden manna,*
>>> *and I will give a white stone,*
>>> *and on the white stone is written a new name*
>>> *that no one knows except the one who receives it.*
>> REVELATION 2:17

ABBA THEODOROS said, "We are not able to keep obsessive thoughts from intruding upon our souls in a disturbing way. But we do have the power to limit the time these troubling ideas may linger within us. We can refuse to allow obsessions to control us. Withdrawal from the world diminishes our obsessions and opens us to the realization of life that is hidden in Christ."

God will give conquerors hidden manna.

It is not good to eat much honey,
or to seek honor on top of honor.
PROVERBS 25:27

BOTH ARSENIUS AND THEODORE OF PHERME disliked fame and praise. Arsenius would avoid anyone who might praise him. Theodore did not avoid them, but the things they said pierced him like knives.

It is not good to eat too much honey.

Let the same mind be in you that was in Christ Jesus, who,
though he was in the form of God, did not regard equality with
God as something to be exploited, but emptied himself, taking
the form of a slave, being born in human likeness. And being
found in human form, he humbled himself and became obedient
to the point of death—even death on a cross.

PHILIPPIANS 2:5–8

ABBA ZENO advised, "Do not live in a famous place. Do not live near anyone who is famous. Do not lay a foundation for your future cell."

Let the same mind be in you
that was in Christ Jesus.

As a deer longs for flowing streams, so my soul longs for you,
O God. My soul thirsts for God, for the living God.
When shall I come and behold the face of God?
PSALM 42:1–2

ABBA POEMEN said, "Desert deer eat many snakes whose venom drives them to look for water with a burning thirst. So it is with monks in the desert. They burn with the venom of demons and can hardly wait for the weekend when they can attend worship, drawing from springs of water in the body and blood of the Lord."

My soul thirsts for God.

For now we see in a mirror, dimly,
but then we will see face to face.
Now I know only in part; then I will know fully,
even as I have been fully known.
1 CORINTHIANS 13:12

EVAGRIUS PONTICUS wrote, "Knowledge is one of our greatest possessions. It works in cooperation with prayer to spur us to divine contemplation."

Now I know only in part.

Joshua fell on his face to the earth and worshiped,
and he said to him,
"What do you command your servant, my lord?"
The commander of the army of the LORD said to Joshua,
"Remove the sandals from your feet,
for the place where you stand is holy."
JOSHUA 5:14–15

A BROTHER asked a hermit if it was good to repent continuously. The hermit answered, "Remember Joshua, the son of Nun. He was prostrate on the ground with his face in the earth when God spoke to him."

The place where you stand is holy.

I will instruct you and teach you the way you should go;
I will counsel you with my eye upon you.
PSALM 32:8

ABBA ARSENIUS, while teaching royalty in the palace, prayed, "Lead me, Lord, in the way of salvation." An inner voice said, "Arsenius, go to a lonely place and you will be saved." After he withdrew to a solitary life, he repeated his prayer. This time, the voice said, "Arsenius, escape. Be silent. Pray continuously. These result in sinlessness."

Lead me, Lord, in the way of salvation.

Thus says the high and lofty one who inhabits eternity,
whose name is Holy: I dwell in the high and holy place,
and also with those who are contrite and humble in spirit,
to revive the spirit of the humble,
and to revive the heart of the contrite.
ISAIAH 57:15

A DESERT HERMIT advised, "Do not blame other people for your troubles. Instead, blame yourself. Think, 'I am in this situation because of my own choices.'"

God dwells with those
who are contrite and humble.

For lack of wood the fire goes out,
and where there is no whisperer, quarreling ceases.
PROVERBS 26:20

A BROTHER asked a hermit, "Abba, if someone brings me gossip, should I ask him to stop speaking?"

"No."

"Why?"

"Because we also gossip. We would be asking someone else to do what we cannot do."

"Then what is the best thing to do?"

"The best thing is to remain silent. Silence is better for us and for others as well."

Where there is no whisperer, quarreling ceases.

Be hospitable to one another without complaining.

1 PETER 4:9

ABBA SILVANUS AND HIS DISCIPLE ZACHARIAS visited a monastery. The monks invited them to share a small meal before they continued their journey. Departing, Zacharias saw a pond by the road and desired a drink of water. Silvanus reminded him that they were observing a fast that day.

Zacharias protested, "But, Abba, we have already broken our fast today."

Silvanus replied, "We ate with them because we love them. Now that we are on our own, let's keep our fast, my son."

Be hospitable to one another.

23 JULY

Beware of the scribes, who like to walk around in long robes,
and to be greeted with respect in the marketplaces, and to have
the best seats in the synagogues and places of honor at banquets!
MARK 12:38–39

A HERMIT said, "I never attempt to climb above my place. It does not bother me to be below others. Instead of worrying about status, I ask God to cleanse me of my unregenerate nature."

I never attempt to climb above my place.

24 JULY

How long will you lie there, O lazybones? When will you rise from your sleep? A little sleep, a little slumber, a little folding of the hands to rest, and poverty will come upon you like a robber, and want, like an armed warrior.

PROVERBS 6:9–11

ABBA POEMEN said, "Smoke drives bees away, allowing us to steal their honey. Idleness drives reverence for God from the soul, exposing its good works to hazards."

When will you rise from your sleep?

25 JULY

*If any want to become my followers, let them deny themselves
and take up their cross daily and follow me. For those who
want to save their life will lose it, and those who lose their life
for my sake will save it. What does it profit them if they gain
the whole world, but lose or forfeit themselves?*

LUKE 9:23–25

EUPREPIUS blessed us with this benediction: May
fear, humility, lack of food and Godly sorrow be
with you.

Take up your cross daily and follow me.

> *Call on me in the day of trouble;*
> *I will deliver you,*
> *and you shall glorify me.*
> PSALM 50:15

A MONK asked an abba for spiritual advice. The abba replied, "Battle furiously!"

But the monk was not satisfied. He said, "Oppressive thoughts trouble me incessantly."

The abba said to him, "Scripture says, 'Call on me in the day of trouble; I will deliver you, and you shall glorify me.' This is clearly stated. Ask God to deliver you from the oppression of your mind."

Ask God to deliver you.

27 JULY

A perverse person spreads strife,
and a whisperer separates close friends.
PROVERBS 16:28

A BBA HYPERICHIUS said, "The serpent whispered to Eve and they were cast out of paradise. If you whisper against your neighbor, you become like the serpent. You condemn the soul of the listener as well as your own."

If you whisper against your neighbor,
you become like the serpent.

It is a credit to you if, being aware of God, you endure pain while suffering unjustly. If you endure when you are beaten for doing wrong, what credit is that? But if you endure when you do right and suffer for it, you have God's approval.

1 PETER 2:19–20

AMMA SARRA said, "If I prayed that everyone should approve my behavior, I would remain forever penitent in front of everyone's door. I do not pray for this. Instead, I ask God for a heart that is pure toward everyone."

Ask God for a heart that is pure.

Now therefore revere the LORD,
and serve him in sincerity and in faithfulness.
JOSHUA 24:14

EVAGRIUS PONTICUS assured us, "If you pray sincerely, you will gain a profound feeling of confidence. Angels will be with you, enlightening you. Pray with appropriate reverence and without fretfulness. Sing with comprehension and give your attention to the details of the music. You will soar like eagles."

Serve the Lord in sincerity and in faithfulness.

The kingdom of heaven may be compared to someone who sowed
good seed in his field; but while everybody was asleep,
an enemy came and sowed weeds among the wheat.

MATTHEW 13:24–25

A BROTHER told Abba Poemen, "If I give someone a piece of bread, the gift becomes worthless because I may have given it to please him."

The hermit responded, "It makes no difference. Even if you did it to please him, you should give him what he needs." Poemen continued with a parable. "There were two farmers. One of them sowed seed, but harvested a poor crop. The other did not sow at all and had no harvest. If famine came, which would be the better off?"

"The one who had planted some seed."

"It is the same for you and me. We sow a few poor seeds, but when famine comes we will not die."

The kingdom of heaven may
be compared to someone who sowed good seed.

I am not worthy of the least of all the steadfast love and all the faithfulness that you have shown your servant.

GENESIS 32:10

WHEN SOMEONE asked a hermit to define humility, he answered, "Humility is when you forgive someone who has wronged you before he expresses regret."

**I am not worthy of the least
of all the steadfast love you have shown.**

> *If we had forgotten the name of our God,*
> *or spread out our hands to a strange god,*
> *would not God discover this?*
> *For he knows the secrets of the heart.*
> PSALM 44:20–21

EVAGRIUS PONTICUS wrote, "The things we say, and bodily motions, are indicators of the soul's passions. Our enemies use these signs to gauge our response to their prompting. Only God, our creator, fully knows our spirit. God does not need any outward symbol to perceive our inner secrets."

Only God, our creator, fully knows our spirit.

> *The eyes of the LORD are on the righteous,*
>   *and his ears are open to their cry.*
> *When the righteous cry for help, the LORD hears,*
>   *and rescues them from all their troubles.*
>   PSALM 34:15, 17

THEODOROS THE ASCETIC said, "Pray night and day. Pray when you are content and pray when you are miserable. Pray with fear and trembling, with an observant and cautious mind. Then your prayer will be acceptable to the Lord."

When the righteous cry for help, the Lord hears.

In him was life, and the life was the light of all people.
JOHN 1:4

ANTONY had everyone's respect. He was considerate of those he visited. An eager learner, he gathered the best traits from others. He copied the self-restraint of one, and the cheerfulness of another. He absorbed gentleness, a love for reading, and the value of nocturnal devotions. He admired one who fasted, praising his determination, and another who slept on the bare ground, honoring his empathy. Antony remembered the love he observed, pondering it and attempting to imitate the best virtues of each person he met. He was never provoked to anger; the only fire that burned in him was a desire to live even better. People called him "God's friend."

**Antony attempted to imitate
the best virtues of each person he met.**

4 AUGUST

You will know them by their fruits. Are grapes gathered from
thorns, or figs from thistles? In the same way, every good tree
bears good fruit, but the bad tree bears bad fruit.
MATTHEW 7:16–17

WHEN SOME MONKS FROM SCETIS visited Amma Sarah, she offered them a little basket of fruit. They selected the poorest fruit to eat, leaving the good for her. Sarah said, "You are truly monks of Scetis."

You will know them by their fruit.

5 AUGUST

Rise, let us be on our way.
JOHN 14:31

ABBA AGATHON and his disciples worked a long time building his cell. When it was completed, he lived in it for about a week, finding it disturbing. He told his disciples he wanted to move on, but they objected. "Why did we work so hard on this if you do not intend to live in it? People will be critical of us, calling us restless and unsettled."

Agathon replied, "A few may express dismay, but others will be edified. They will call us blessed, observing that we are moving for God's sake and willingly abandon our belongings. I am going. Come with me if you wish."

His disciples bowed low and asked to accompany him.

Rise, let us be on our way.

Then Jesus was led up by the Spirit
into the wilderness to be tempted by the devil.
MATTHEW 4:1

ABBA POEMEN believed that the only time you could observe a person's true character was when that person was tempted.

Observe a person's true character.

7 AUGUST

Praise the LORD with the lyre;
make melody to him with the harp of ten strings.
Sing to him a new song;
play skillfully on the strings,
with loud shouts.
PSALM 33:2–3

MACARIUS THE GREAT said, "The Spirit sings a new song to the Lord when it takes possession of a soul. With the strings of the body and the lyre of the soul, the Spirit chants praise to the life-giving Christ. In the same way that breath makes music when blown through a flute, the Holy Spirit harmonizes in the holy saints who sing hymns and psalms to God with a pure heart."

Sing to him a new song.

Do not be carried away by all kinds of strange teachings.
HEBREWS 13:9

MALICIOUS skeptics visited Abba Agathon to see if they could annoy him. They had heard that Agathon possessed great discretion and self-control. They spoke directly to him, "Agathon, we heard that you are an adulterer and full of pride."

He answered, "Yes, that's true."

"Are you the same Agathon who gossips and slanders?"

"I am."

"Are you Agathon the heretic?"

"No, I am not a heretic."

"Why did you patiently endure it when we slandered you, but refuse to be called a heretic?"

Agathon answered, "Your first accusations were good for my soul, but to be a heretic is to be separated from God. I do not want to be apart from God."

I do not want to be apart from God.

Join in imitating me,
and observe those who live according to
the example you have in us.

PHILIPPIANS 3:17

SOMEONE expressed personal concern to Abba Paesius. "I am worried about my soul. I have no spiritual awareness and I do not fear God."

Paesius answered, "Find someone who does fear God. Move in with him. By living with him you will learn to fear God."

Find someone who fears God.

Should the wise answer with windy knowledge,
and fill themselves with the east wind?
Should they argue in unprofitable talk,
or in words with which they can do no good?

JOB 15:2–3

AMMA THEODORA commented regarding overheard conversations. "In the same way that you pick and choose among dishes at a banquet with many courses, you may listen to secular conversations near you while having your heart focused on God. As certain foods do not appeal to your palate, there are topics of conversation that will bring you no pleasure. No harm will be done."

Should the wise argue in unprofitable talk?

Pray that you may not come into the time of trial;
the spirit indeed is willing, but the flesh is weak.
MATTHEW 26:41

Evagrius Ponticus wrote, "We do not have a commandment to work and to devote the night to vigils and to fast constantly, but we are required to pray without ceasing. While our weak bodies are not up to such disciplines that restore health to our souls, labor, vigils, and fasting do involve physical cooperation. Prayer is a spiritual discipline that strengthens the soul. Prayer fights for us even without the participation of the flesh."

The spirit is willing, but the flesh is weak.

12 AUGUST

Be silent before the Lord GOD!
For the day of the LORD is at hand;
the LORD has prepared a sacrifice,
he has consecrated his guests.

ZEPHANIAH 1:7

ABBA MOSES asked the dying monk Zacharias what
he could see.
Zacharias said, "Silence is best, Abba."
Moses agreed, "Yes, my son, keep silent."

The day of the Lord is at hand.

13 AUGUST

Then the woman came and told her husband, "A man of God came to me, and his appearance was like that of an angel of God, most awe-inspiring; I did not ask him where he came from, and he did not tell me his name."

JUDGES 13:6

THE DESERT HERMITS taught, "If you actually see an angel, do not accept it casually. Humbly remind yourself that while you live in sin and are not worthy to see an angel, the gift may still be given to you."

If you see an angel, do not accept it casually.

By your endurance you will gain your souls.
LUKE 21:19

W HEN SOME BROTHERS visited a desert hermit, they found foul-mouthed shepherds tending sheep outside the hermitage. "Why do you permit those boys to be out there?" they asked. "Abba, why don't you ask them to stop cussing with each other?"

The hermit said, "There have been moments when I almost spoke to them, but I restrained myself. If I can't endure something small like this language, how will I resist a serious temptation if God permits one to come to me? Therefore, I remain silent. I am trying to learn how to bear whatever comes my way."

By endurance you will gain your soul.

God has shown me that I should not call
anyone profane or unclean.
ACTS 10:28

A CHURCH ELDER would visit a hermit and consecrate the Eucharist for him. Someone reported bad things about that elder to the hermit. The next time he came, the hermit refused to let him in. Then the hermit heard a voice saying, "Men have usurped the judgment of God." In a vision, he saw a leper lifting a golden bucket on a golden rope from a golden well. The water was abundant and the hermit was thirsty, but he would not accept any water because of the leper. The voice spoke again, "Why won't you drink this water? Does it matter who draws it? All he is doing is pouring it out for you." The hermit understood the significance of the vision and asked the elder to return.

Call no one unclean.

They asked him, "What then? Are you Elijah?"
He said, "I am not." "Are you the prophet?" He answered, "No."
Then they said to him, "Who are you? Let us have an answer
for those who sent us. What do you say about yourself?"
JOHN 1:21–22

ABBA SISOIS lived on the mountain of Antony. A visiting brother asked him, "Abba, are you the equal of Antony?"

Sisois replied, "If I had even one thought like Antony, I would leap toward heaven as a flame. I know I must struggle to keep my thoughts under control."

What do you say about yourself?

Is such the fast that I choose, a day to humble oneself?
    Is it to bow down the head like a bulrush,
       and to lie in sackcloth and ashes?
      Will you call this a fast, a day acceptable to the LORD?
    ISAIAH 58:5

A BROTHER was hungry at dawn, but he struggled not to eat until nine o'clock. At nine o'clock, he decided to put off eating until noon. At noon, he dipped a piece of bread and sat down to eat, but thought, "No, I will wait until three." At three o'clock, he prayed and saw the devil departing like smoke. His hunger was controlled.

Will you call this a fast,
    a day acceptable to the Lord?

Guard what has been entrusted to you. Avoid the profane chatter and contradictions of what is falsely called knowledge; by professing it some have missed the mark as regards the faith.

1 TIMOTHY 6:20

PALLADIUS said of Amma Melania, "She enjoyed reading and was well-educated. Turning night into day, she read all the works of earlier Christians: three million lines by Origen and a quarter of a million lines by Gregory, Stephen, Pierius, Basil, and others. This was not casual reading, but fervent study. Melania read each book seven or eight times, rising above false knowledge. Her reading gave her spirit wings on which she could fly to Christ."

Guard what has been entrusted to you.

19 AUGUST

We are God's servants, working together.
1 CORINTHIANS 3:9

ONE DESERT HERMIT was visiting another. The host asked his disciple, "Make us some lentil soup, my son." After the disciple prepared the soup, the hermit said, "Dip a little bread in it for us." He dipped the bread, but the two engrossed hermits continued their religious conversation until noon the next day.

The host hermit then turned to his disciple and said, "Make us some lentil soup, my son." The young man replied that he had made it yesterday, so they got up and ate the soup.

We are God's servants.

Truly it is the spirit in a mortal, the breath of the Almighty,
that makes for understanding. It is not the old that are wise,
nor the aged that understand what is right.

JOB 32:8–9

A HERMIT said, "If you want to live in the desert, you
need to be a teacher rather than a learner. If you still
need teaching, you will get into trouble."

Understanding is a spiritual gift.

To watch over mouth and tongue is to keep out of trouble.
PROVERBS 21:23

SOME BROTHERS from Scetis took a voyage to see Antony. They met an old man on board the ship who was also on his way to Antony. During the trip, they discussed the sayings of the Fathers, the Holy Scriptures, and the kind of manual labor they did. The old man listened, but did not speak.

Antony greeted them, saying, "You had a good companion on your journey in this old man." Then he spoke to the old man, "You traveled with good brothers."

The old man said, "Yes, they are good, but their house does not have a door. Anyone can enter and steal." He believed they talked too much, saying the first thing they thought.

Watch over mouth and tongue.

22 AUGUST

You have dealt well with your servant,
O LORD, according to your word.
Teach me good judgment and knowledge,
for I believe in your commandments.
PSALM 119:65–66

ANTONY said, "Some ruin their bodies through fasting improperly. This lack of discretion separates them even more from God."

Teach me good judgment and knowledge.

David said longingly, "O that someone would give me water to drink from the well of Bethlehem that is by the gate!"

2 SAMUEL 23:15

MARK told Arsenius, "I saw a brother setting out cabbages. Isn't it better to have nothing unnecessary?"

Arsenius replied, "Yes, that's better, but each one of us should do what seems right for our individual needs. If the brother lacks the strength to live without his cabbages, let him grow them."

**Each one should do what seems right
for our individual needs.**

I fear that when I come,
I may find you not as I wish,
and that you may find me not as you wish;
I fear that there may perhaps be quarreling,
jealousy, anger, selfishness,
slander, gossip, conceit, and disorder.
2 CORINTHIANS 12:20

A HERMIT advised, "If someone speaks to you about a controversy, do not argue with him. If what he says makes sense, say, 'Yes.' If his comments are misguided, say, 'I don't know anything about that.' If you refuse to dispute with his ideas, your mind will be at peace."

Refuse to dispute and your mind will be at peace.

I appeal to you therefore, brothers and sisters, by the mercies of God, to present your bodies as a living sacrifice, holy and acceptable to God, which is your spiritual worship.

ROMANS 12:1

EVAGRIUS PONTICUS wrote, "If you want to pray in the spirit, use nothing from the flesh. This will prevent a cloud from obscuring your sight when you pray. Trust God to provide what your body needs. Then it will become evident that you also trust God for the needs of your spirit."

Present your body as a living sacrifice.

Jesus took with him Peter and John and James,
and went up on the mountain to pray.
And while he was praying,
the appearance of his face changed,
and his clothes became dazzling white.
LUKE 9:28–29

OTHERS report that unless Abba Sisois quickly lowered his hands when he stood up to pray, his mind would become preoccupied with heaven. Therefore, if he were praying with a companion, he would soon drop his hands and end his prayer. He did not want to become enraptured or to continue praying too long for the other person to endure.

While he was praying,
the appearance of his face changed.

27 AUGUST

Those who are spiritual discern all things, and they are
themselves subject to no one else's scrutiny. "For who has known
the mind of the LORD so as to instruct him?"
But we have the mind of Christ.
1 CORINTHIANS 2:15–16

THEOPHILUS, ARCHBISHOP OF ALEXANDRIA, visited Scetis. The brothers urged Abba Pambo to speak to the bishop in order to edify him. Pambo replied, "If my silence does not edify him, there is nothing he can learn from my speech."

Have the mind of Christ.

28 AUGUST

Those who are far from you, [Lord,] will perish;
you put an end to those who are false to you. But for me it is
good to be near God; I have made the Lord GOD my refuge,
to tell of all your works.
PSALM 73:27–28

ABBA MATHOIS said, "The closer we come to God, the more clearly we perceive that we are sinners. The prophet Isaiah saw the Lord and understood that he himself was wretched and unclean."

It is good to be near God.

When my soul was embittered, when I was pricked in heart,
I was stupid and ignorant; I was like a brute beast toward you.
Nevertheless I am continually with you;
you hold my right hand.
PSALM 73:21–23

ABBA POEMEN asked Nesteros how he controlled himself so well. "If there is a problem among the brothers at the monastery you keep silent and remain at peace."

Nesteros was reluctant to answer. After repeated urging he said, "Abba, when I first became a part of the community I said to my soul, 'You must be like a donkey. A donkey makes no comment when it is beaten. That is the way you must behave, as the psalm directs.'"

You hold my right hand.

Welcome one another, therefore,
just as Christ has welcomed you, for the glory of God.
ROMANS 15:7

Two BROTHERS visited a hermit who made it a habit not to eat every day. The hermit welcomed them warmly, showing complete hospitality. Smiling, he said, "Fasting has its own reward, but when love motivates you to eat, you keep two commandments. You lose your self-will and you refresh your brothers."

Welcome one another
as Christ has welcomed you.

*Cast away from you all the transgressions
that you have committed against me,
and get yourselves a new heart and a new spirit!
Why will you die?*
EZEKIEL 18:31

A HERMIT said, "When we first began to meet with each other in the assembly for healthy spiritual discussion, we were always apart from the world and close to heaven. Now when we meet we do little more than gossip, dragging ourselves down."

Get a new heart and a new spirit.

You open your hand,
satisfying the desire of every living thing.
PSALM 145:16

A HERMIT said, "One person may eat a lot and still be hungry. Another eats only a little and is satisfied. The one who remains hungry after eating a lot obtains more merit than the one who is satisfied with a little."

God satisfies the desire of every living thing.

Are there not twelve hours of daylight?
Those who walk during the day do not stumble,
because they see the light of this world.
But those who walk at night stumble,
because the light is not in them.
JOHN 11:9–10

AMMA ALEXANDRA reported, "Early in the morning I weave cloth while reciting the Psalms and praying. Then I think of the holy fathers and ponder the lives of prophets, apostles, and martyrs. The rest of the day I do manual labor, eat some bread, and receive comfort as I live the remainder of my life with positive thoughts."

Those who walk during the day do not stumble.

All who believed were together
and had all things in common;
they would sell their possessions and
goods and distribute the proceeds to all,
as any had need.
ACTS 2:44–45

A BASKET-MAKING MONK was putting handles on his work when he overheard a nearby monk fretting. "What will I do? The trader will be here soon and I don't have any handles to put on my baskets." The first monk began to remove the handles he had put on his own baskets and delivered them to the other. He said, "I don't need these. Please use them on your baskets." He then helped the brother finish his baskets while leaving his own without handles.

**All who believed were together
and had all things in common.**

4 SEPTEMBER

You, then, that teach others, will you not teach yourself?
ROMANS 2:21

AMMA THEODORA lists these qualities for a teacher:
Have no desire to dominate.
Have no interest in vanity and pride.
Never be distracted by flattery or gifts.
Be in control of the stomach.
Be slow to become angry.
Be as patient, gentle, and humble as possible.
Be properly examined and without political ties.
Be a lover of souls.

**You, then, that teach others,
will you not teach yourself?**

For he will command his angels concerning you to guard you in
all your ways. On their hands they will bear you up,
so that you will not dash your foot against a stone.
PSALM 91:11–12

EVAGRIUS PONTICUS wrote, "God's holy angels encourage us to pray. They are present among us and enjoy praying for us. When we carelessly allow distracting thoughts during our prayers, we disturb the angels. They are fighting for us while we fail to take care of our part with God. This shows contempt of their services and our turning away from God, which is exactly what the impure demons want."

God's holy angels encourage us to pray.

6 SEPTEMBER

Jesus increased in wisdom and in years,
and in divine and human favor.
LUKE 2:52

WHEN ABBA PAMBO was near death and his friends were standing around him, he said, "Since I began to live in solitude, I have no memory of ever having eaten anything I did not labor for. Neither have I spoken any words I regret. But now, as I go to the Lord, I realize I have not even begun to serve God."

I have not even begun to serve God.

Jesus took the loaves, and when he had given thanks,
he distributed them to those who were seated;
so also the fish, as much as they wanted.
When they were satisfied, he told his disciples,
"Gather up the fragments left over,
so that nothing may be lost."
JOHN 6:11–12

DANIEL reported that they lived near Abba Arsenius. "Every year we would give him a little food, about enough to last him a year. Every time we returned for a visit, he would share some of it with us."

He distributed them [the bread and the fish]
to those who were seated.

As you have always obeyed me, not only in my presence, but much more now in my absence, work out your own salvation with fear and trembling; for it is God who is at work in you, enabling you both to will and to work for his good pleasure.

PHILIPPIANS 2:12–13

ABBA EVAGRIUS said, "When your attention wanders, pray. As Paul wrote, pray with fear and trembling, sincerely and carefully. This is the way we should pray, because evil forces are attempting to hold us back."

God is at work in you.

Confident of your obedience,
I am writing to you,
knowing that you will do even more than I say.

PHILEMON 1:21

FOUR MONKS FROM SCETIS, wearing tunics of animal hide, visited Abba Pambo. In private, each monk told Pambo of the virtues of another. One was a diligent faster, another did not own anything, the third was extraordinarily charitable, and the fourth had lived obedient to others for twenty-two years.

Pambo said, "The fourth monk has the greatest virtue. The rest of you use your own will to fulfill your promises, but he has rooted out self-will and become the servant of the will of others. Such a person will be a saint if such obedience continues until death."

You will do even more than I say.

When you come together, it is not really to eat the Lord's supper.
For when the time comes to eat, each of you goes ahead with your
own supper, and one goes hungry and another becomes drunk.

1 CORINTHIANS 11:20–21

ABBA ISAIAH reported that during an agape dinner, brothers engaged in conversation. The priest of Pelusia corrected them, saying, "Be quiet, brothers. I notice that one eating and drinking with you is praying. His prayers ascend to the presence of God like fire."

One eating and drinking with you is praying.

Will not God grant justice to his chosen ones who cry to him day and night? Will he delay long in helping them? I tell you, he will quickly grant justice to them.
LUKE 18:7–8

EVAGRIUS PONTICUS wrote, "Our Lord told a parable regarding the necessity of constant prayer that is not discouraged. If you do not receive what you are seeking, do not become despondent. Remain courageous. God will answer your prayer. God will render justice to those who cry out to him night and day. Continue to pray as a ship sailing with all its sails unfurled."

**God will render justice
to those who cry out to him.**

Love is strong as death,

passion fierce as the grave.

SONG OF SOLOMON 8:6

A REVERED AND FAMOUS HERMIT lived in Egypt before Abba Poemen went there. When Poemen arrived with his monks, many people switched their interest and support to him. The hermit became jealous and openly criticized the new arrivals. Poemen regretted this and asked his monks what they could do. "We are suffering because of these people who left him and came to us. We are not worth their attention. Let's try to do something to help that hermit. Prepare some food and get a little jug of wine. We will visit him and attempt to soothe his feelings."

When they knocked at the hermit's cell, his disciple asked who they were. "Tell the abba that Poemen is here seeking his blessing."

The hermit sent the disciple back to the door to say, "I am busy. Please go away." They declined to depart until they had received the hermit's blessing.

Observing their humility and resolve, the hermit relented. They entered and shared the food they had brought. As they ate, the offended hermit said to Poemen, "I have not been told the full truth about you. You are a hundred times better than I had heard." They became good friends from that moment.

Love is strong as death.

There is no longer Jew or Greek,
there is no longer slave or free,
there is no longer male and female;
for all of you are one in Christ Jesus.
— GALATIANS 3:28

TWO MONKS FROM PELUSIUM went to see Amma Sarah, intending to humiliate her. They told her not to be proud because they had come to consult a woman. She told them her body was female, but not her soul.

All are one in Christ Jesus.

And whenever you fast, do not look dismal, like the hypocrites,
for they disfigure their faces so as to show others that they are
fasting. Truly I tell you, they have received their reward.
MATTHEW 6:16

ABBA MATHOIS advised a brother, "Do not attempt to become an eccentric character by letting the word get out that you are independent and refuse to eat one thing or another. This will quickly gain you a little reputation, but it will bring you grief. Crowds of people will invade your peace."

Gain a little reputation and it will bring you grief.

Take the shield of faith,
with which you will be able to quench
all the flaming arrows of the evil one.
Take the helmet of salvation,
and the sword of the Spirit,
which is the word of God.
EPHESIANS 6:16–17

EVAGRIUS PONTICUS wrote, "If you are genuinely interested in prayer, expect to be assaulted by demonic forces. Patiently endure the lashes you will receive. You will be attacked as though by a wild beast, and your entire body will be involved."

Take the shield of faith.

16 SEPTEMBER

Samson went down with his father and mother to Timnah.
When he came to the vineyards of Timnah,
suddenly a young lion roared at him. The spirit of the LORD
rushed on him and he tore the lion apart barehanded
as one might tear apart a kid.

JUDGES 14:5–6

EVAGRIUS PONTICUS wrote, "Train for prayer the way an athlete trains for competition. Learn not to let some unexpected threatening vision create anxiety in you. Regardless of the hideous nature of the troubling images, stand firm. If you witness to your faith this way you can face your spiritual enemies with confidence."

**Train for prayer the way
an athlete trains for competition.**

Some wandered in desert wastes,
finding no way to an inhabited town;
hungry and thirsty, their soul fainted within them.
Then they cried to the LORD in their trouble,
and he delivered them from their distress;
he led them by a straight way,
until they reached an inhabited town.
Let them thank the LORD for his steadfast love,
for his wonderful works to humankind.
For he satisfies the thirsty,
and the hungry he fills with good things.
PSALM 107:4–9

EVAGRIUS PONTICUS wrote, "If you endure painful moments you will arrive some day at consolation. The one who remains strong in disagreeable times will also have pleasant times."

For he satisfies the thirsty.

Pray in the Spirit at all times in every prayer and supplication.
To that end keep alert and always persevere in
supplication for all the saints.
EPHESIANS 6:18

EVAGRIUS PONTICUS wrote, "Do not allow evil demons to lead you astray. The wise thing to do is to turn to God in prayer. Ask him to make it clear to you whether or not he has inspired an idea. If it turns out to be from an evil source, ask God to drive it out of your mind. Then be brave. The dog will back off. Your prayer will drive him away with divine lashings you can't perceive."

The wise thing to do is to turn to God in prayer.

19 SEPTEMBER

The LORD is my shepherd, I shall not want.
He makes me lie down in green pastures;
he leads me beside still waters; he restores my soul.
He leads me in right paths for his name's sake.
PSALM 23:1–3

AMMA MACRINA gave exclusive attention to God through constant prayer and chanting of the Psalms night and day. It was both work and rest.

The Lord is my shepherd, I shall not want.

Those who live according to the flesh set their minds on the things of the flesh, but those who live according to the Spirit set their minds on the things of the Spirit.

ROMANS 8:5

B ENJAMIN, A PRIEST IN CELLIA, reported that a group of brothers visited a hermit in Scetis and offered to give him some oil. The hermit pointed to a little jar on a shelf and said, "Look, there is the oil you brought me three years ago. I have left it where you put it." Benjamin said the hermit's austerity was remarkable.

Set your mind on the things of the Spirit.

He [God] has blinded their eyes and hardened their heart,
so that they might not look with their eyes.
JOHN 12:40

A HERMIT said, "The miller must blindfold a donkey working the treadmill. If he does not, it will eat the grain. Merciful God has blindfolded us to prevent us from noticing anything good we do. Otherwise, we might be proud of ourselves and forfeit our reward. God permits us to see our own bad thoughts because then we will regret them and censure ourselves. These negative thoughts are the cloth of our blindfolds that keep any goodness out of sight. If you accuse yourself, you keep your reward."

Pride forfeits our reward.

We brought nothing into the world,
so that we can take nothing out of it.
1 TIMOTHY 6:7

WHEN MACARIUS lived in Egypt, he returned to his cell one day to discover a thief with a donkey who was stealing his belongings. Pretending that he was not the owner, Macarius helped the thief load his donkey and sent him on his way with a smile. He thought, "We bring nothing into this world. The Lord gives and the Lord takes away. Blessed be the name of the Lord."

The Lord gives and the Lord takes away.

23 SEPTEMBER

Come with us, and we will treat you well.

NUMBERS 10:29

A HERMIT reported a ritual performed by the early fathers. "They would call upon new brothers who attempted to live a solitary life. If they met someone experiencing severe temptation, they would lead him to church. There they would fill a water basin and offer prayers on behalf of the tempted brother. Then all of the monks would wash their hands in the basin and pour the water over the struggling brother. This would immediately free him."

Pray for one who is tempted.

We are debtors, not to the flesh, to live according to the flesh—
for if you live according to the flesh, you will die; but if by the
Spirit you put to death the deeds of the body, you will live.
For all who are led by the Spirit of God are children of God.
ROMANS 8:12–14

ABBA DANIEL taught that the soul prospers in direct
proportion to the weakening of the body.

All who are led
by the Spirit of God are children of God.

When will the new moon be over so that we may sell grain;
and the sabbath, so that we may offer wheat for sale? We will
make the ephah small and the shekel great, and practice deceit
with false balances, buying the poor for silver and the needy for
a pair of sandals, and selling the sweepings of the wheat.
AMOS 8:5–6

AMMA SYNCLETICA said, "Merchants work hard for money, often endangering their lives on the high seas. The more they make, the more they want. They consider what they have is not enough, continually searching for a way to increase their inventory. But we possess nothing, not even the things most people consider essential. With reverence for God, we try to get along with as little as possible."

With reverence for God,
we try to get along with as little as possible.

Come to me, all you that are weary
and are carrying heavy burdens,
and I will give you rest.
Take my yoke upon you, and learn from me;
for I am gentle and humble in heart,
and you will find rest for your souls.
For my yoke is easy, and my burden is light.
MATTHEW 11:28–30

ABBA HYPERICHIUS said, "Sing hymns of praise to God and meditate continuously. This will weaken the power of temptations. A traveler with a heavy burden will frequently pause for rest along the way. This makes the journey easier and the burden lighter."

For my yoke is easy, and my burden is light.

Do not worry about your life, what you will eat or what you
will drink, or about your body, what you will wear.
Is not life more than food, and the body more than clothing?
Look at the birds of the air; they neither sow nor reap nor
gather into barns, and yet your heavenly Father feeds them.
Are you not of more value than they? And can any of you by
worrying add a single hour to your span of life?
And why do you worry about clothing?
Consider the lilies of the field, how they grow;
they neither toil nor spin, yet I tell you,
even Solomon in all his glory was not clothed like one of these.
MATTHEW 6:25–29

EUPREPIUS gave this directive: Eat straw, wear straw, sleep on straw. Have no fondness for material things. Instead, try to obtain a heart of iron.

Consider the lilies of the field.

28 SEPTEMBER

In returning and rest you shall be saved;
in quietness and in trust shall be your strength.

ISAIAH 30:15

WHEN WORSHIP ENDED, MACARIUS THE GREAT told the brothers in Scetis, "Run away!" One of the brothers asked him, "Abba, where shall we go? We already live in the desert."

Macarius touched his lips with his finger and said, "This is what we must flee." Then he entered his cell, closed the door, and remained alone.

In quietness and in trust shall be your strength.

> *Do not repay anyone evil for evil,*
> *but take thought for what is noble in the sight of all.*
> ROMANS 12:17

Evagrius Ponticus wrote, "You can count on it: when you do something good for someone, another person will treat you badly. The demons use this to induce you to strike out while protesting injustice. The moment you succumb, you will spill what you have carefully harvested. Beware of this."

Take thought for what is noble in the sight of all.

*Martha was distracted by her many tasks; so she came to him
and asked, "Lord, do you not care that my sister has left me to
do all the work by myself? Tell her then to help me."*
LUKE 10:40

A DESERT SOLITARY, dear to God and often in prayer, was joined by two angels as he walked, one on each side. He tried to give them no attention. He did not want to be distracted from his conversation with Christ.

Let nothing distract you from Christ.

Blessed are the poor in spirit,
for theirs is the kingdom of heaven.
MATTHEW 5:3

EVAGRIUS said, "Blessed is the spirit that can pray without distraction and has an increasing desire for God. Blessed is the spirit that is unencumbered by anything physical during a time of prayer. Blessed is the spirit that is unaware of everything other than prayer. Blessed is the person who considers himself less than dirt. Blessed is the monk who enjoys the progress of another as much as his own."

Blessed are the poor in spirit.

What are mortals, that they can be clean? Or those born of
woman, that they can be righteous? God puts no trust even in
his holy ones, and the heavens are not clean in his sight.

JOB 15:14–15

SOME BROTHERS approached Abba Zeno and asked him to interpret a text from the book of Job, which states that the heavens are not clean in God's sight. He began by saying, "You have ceased observing your sins, and now you are searching heavenly regions."

Then he said, "The text means that God alone is pure. Heaven itself is not clean in God's sight."

God alone is pure.

3 OCTOBER

It is what comes out of a person that defiles. For it is from within, from the human heart, that evil intentions come: fornication, theft, murder, adultery, avarice, wickedness, deceit, licentiousness, envy, slander, pride, folly. All these evil things come from within, and they defile a person.

MARK 7:20–23

AMMA SYNCLETICA reminded us, "Many who retreat to the mountains live as though they were in town. They waste their time. A solitary may live with crowded personal thoughts."

It is what comes out of a person that defiles.

Then Peter came and said to him, "Lord, if another member of the church sins against me, how often should I forgive? As many as seven times?" Jesus said to him, "Not seven times, but, I tell you, seventy-seven times."

MATTHEW 18:21–22

ONE OF THE GREAT HERMITS had a standard answer for those who sought his advice. He would say with great self-assurance, "Listen, I am performing God's work for him, sitting in God's judgment seat. What may I do for you? If you say to me, 'Have mercy on me,' God says to you, 'I will have mercy on you only if you have mercy on your brothers. If you want me to forgive you, you must forgive others.' Is God therefore the source of your guilt? Of course not! It is in your control, whether you do or do not wish to be saved."

**It is in your control,
whether you do or do not wish to be saved.**

5 OCTOBER

Do not be afraid, little flock,
for it is your Father's good pleasure to give you the kingdom.
Sell your possessions, and give alms.
Make purses for yourselves that do not wear out,
an unfailing treasure in heaven,
where no thief comes near and no moth destroys.
For where your treasure is, there your heart will be also.

LUKE 12:32–34

ABBA HYPERICHIUS said, "Keep your mind constantly on the kingdom of heaven, and you will soon inherit it."

**For where your treasure is,
there your heart will be also.**

If only we had meat to eat! We remember the fish we used to eat

in Egypt for nothing, the cucumbers, the melons, the leeks, the

onions, and the garlic; but now our strength is dried up, and

there is nothing at all but this manna to look at.

NUMBERS 11:4–6

EVAGRIUS PONTICUS wrote, "A prisoner in chains cannot run. Neither can a mind incarcerated by emotion discover the place of spiritual prayer. Impassioned thoughts abuse it roughly. It cannot be resolute and serene."

**A mind incarcerated by emotion
cannot discover spiritual prayer.**

Since there will never cease to be some in need on the earth,
I therefore command you,
"Open your hand to the poor and needy neighbor in your land."
DEUTERONOMY 15:11

A N OLD MAN who lived at Turres ardently practiced holy poverty and almsgiving. When a beggar approached his cell asking alms, the old man brought out the only thing he had—a single loaf of bread. The beggar said, "I don't want bread. I need clothes."

The old man, wanting to comfort him, took his hand and led him into his cell, which was empty. The beggar, seeing nothing and touched by the old man's goodness, opened his wallet, and dumped everything he had on the floor. He said, "Take these, good abba. I will ask somewhere else for what I need."

Open your hand to the poor and needy.

Bless the LORD, O my soul, and all that is within me, bless his holy name. Bless the LORD, O my soul, and do not forget all his benefits—who forgives all your iniquity, who heals all your diseases, who redeems your life from the Pit, who crowns you with steadfast love and mercy, who satisfies you with good as long as you live so that your youth is renewed like the eagle's.

PSALM 103:1–5

ANTONY THE GREAT said, "Think about God all the time."

Bless the Lord, O my soul.

Give liberally and be ungrudging when you do so,
for on this account the LORD your God will bless you
in all your work and in all that you undertake.

DEUTERONOMY 15:10

AN OLD MAN who lived in the monastery at Cuziba would patrol the road from the Jordan River to Jerusalem, carrying bread and water. If he saw anyone growing tired, he would shoulder his load and carry it as far as the Mount of Olives. On the way back down, he would carry travelers' burdens as far as Jericho. Sometimes you could see the old man sweating under a huge bundle. At other times, you might see him carrying a child or two on his shoulder. He repaired broken shoes of men and women because he carried supplies to do that. He would give a drink of water to some and a taste of bread to others. If he encountered anyone naked, he would give him the clothes off his back. If he came upon a corpse, he would recite psalms and prayers before burying the body.

Give liberally and be ungrudging when you do so.

10 OCTOBER

Whoever welcomes you welcomes me,
and whoever welcomes me welcomes the one who sent me.
MATTHEW 10:40

* * * * * * *

RUFINUS OF AQUILEIA wrote, "I visited Nitria, the most famous monastery in Egypt, about thirty-seven miles from Alexandria. The brothers there live in approximately fifty scattered dwellings. When they saw us coming, they came out of their cells like a swarm of bees, running to meet us cheerfully with water and bread.

"After they had welcomed us, they took us to church, chanting psalms. They washed our feet and dried them with the linen they wore. This act not only removed the dust of the road, but also seemed to purge the stains of mortal life.

"Their warm, human courtesy is beyond description. I have never seen love so much in flower, and neither have I seen such meditation upon Scripture and application of sacred learning."

If I welcome others, I welcome Christ.

They went to a place called Gethsemane; and he said to his disciples, "Sit here while I pray."

MARK 14:32

EVAGRIUS PONTICUS wrote, "As your spirit gradually withdraws from your body when you have an ardent desire for God, ignoring all ideas that are prompted by sensual awareness and temperament, becoming reverent and joyful, you may then be certain that you are getting close to the territory named prayer."

An ardent desire for God is close to prayer.

I have become like one who,
after the summer fruit has been gathered,
after the vintage has been gleaned,
finds no cluster to eat.
MICAH 7:1

ABBA MACARIUS received a bunch of grapes from a brother. Love made him think of others rather than himself, so he carried the grapes to another brother who seemed to be feebler. The sick hermit thanked God for the way Macarius had thought of him, but he also thought more of others than of himself. He took the grapes to another, who passed it on to another, until the bunch of grapes made the rounds of all the cells. Because the cells were scattered and far apart in the desert and no one knew who had given them first, the grapes eventually returned to Macarius. This circle of love inspired Macarius to seek sterner discipline in his spiritual life.

What you give away returns to you.

This poor soul cried, and was heard by the LORD,
and was saved from every trouble.

PSALM 34:6

EVAGRIUS said, "If you are bothered by a distracting thought, it is not helpful to thrash around in your prayer about it. Simply repent. This will give your spiritual sword a sharper edge."

This poor soul cried, and was heard by the Lord.

Whatever your hand finds to do, do with your might; for there is no work or thought or knowledge or wisdom in Sheol, to which you are going. ECCLESIASTES 9:10

ABBA PAUL lived in the vast desert of Porphyrio, more than seven days from any inhabited place. This made the simplest agricultural commerce impractical. Still, he gathered palm leaves and worked with them every day as though he were earning his living. When his cave filled annually with the product of his hands, he would take it outside and burn it. He proved that unless a monk works with his hands he would not survive a solitary life in the desert; neither could he advance any higher in holiness. Though such work may not be necessary, do it for the cleansing of the heart, for disciplining thought, for perseverance in the cell, and for defeating boredom.

**Whatever your hand finds to do,
do with your might.**

15 OCTOBER

"Master, did you not sow good seed in your field?
Where, then, did these weeds come from?" He answered,
"An enemy has done this."
MATTHEW 13:27–28

ABBA MATHOIS said, "Satan has no knowledge of which passion will seduce a particular soul; therefore, he scatters a wide variety of weeds. Without discretion, he tosses seeds of lust, slander, and all the rest. If he notices an individual who is particularly attracted toward one, he concentrates on that. If Satan knew the best temptation for each soul, he would not sow such a variety."

Where did these weeds come from?

As the eyes of servants look to
the hand of their master,
as the eyes of a maid to the hand of her mistress,
so our eyes look to the LORD *our God,*
until he has mercy upon us.
PSALM 123:2

EVAGRIUS PONTICUS wrote, "If you seriously desire true prayer and yet succumb to anger or resentment, you are out of your mind. If you want to see clearly, you do not scratch your eyes."

Our eyes look to the Lord our God.

[Jesus] looked up and saw rich people putting their gifts into the treasury; he also saw a poor widow put in two small copper coins. He said, "Truly I tell you, this poor widow has put in more than all of them; for all of them have contributed out of their abundance, but she out of her poverty has put in all she had to live on."

LUKE 21:1–4

LADY MELANIA traveled from Rome to Alexandria to visit the highly respected Abba Pambo in the desert. She offered him a chest containing three hundred pounds of silver. She reported, "He was sitting there weaving a basket and blessed me with a simple, 'May God reward you.' He then gave instructions for distributing it among the poorest monasteries."

She stood there, expecting a comment from Pambo regarding her gift. When he said nothing, she spoke, "I want you to know, Abba, there are three hundred pounds of silver in that chest."

Without looking up, Pambo said, "My daughter, God has no need to learn the bulk of your gift. He who weighs the mountains knows far better than you its weight. If you were giving it to me, it would be important to report. But you did not bring it to me, but to God, who respected an offering of two pennies. Peace, be still."

God has no need to learn the bulk of your gift.

When you are offering your gift at the altar, if you remember
that your brother or sister has something against you, leave
your gift there before the altar and go; first be reconciled to your
brother or sister, and then come and offer your gift.
MATTHEW 5:23–24

M ACARIUS said, "If we remember the evil that others
have done to us, we shut down our ability to
remember God."

First be reconciled.

The place is too crowded for me;
make room for me to settle.

ISAIAH 49:20

A BBA ARSENIUS lived in a cell that was thirty miles away from the others. He usually did not wander far. When the monks had to abandon Scetis, Arsenius went away weeping. He said, "The world destroyed Rome, and now too many monks have destroyed Scetis."

Make room for me to settle.

Whenever you pray, do not be like the hypocrites; for they love to stand and pray in the synagogues and at the street corners, so that they may be seen by others. Truly I tell you, they have received their reward. But whenever you pray, go into your room and shut the door and pray to your Father who is in secret; and your Father who sees in secret will reward you.

MATTHEW 6:5–6

Evagrius Ponticus wrote, "If you really want to pray, keep away from everything that hinders prayer. Then when God approaches you, he merely needs to accompany you."

Pray to your Father who is in secret.

A lawyer asked him a question to test him. "Teacher, which commandment in the law is the greatest?" He said to him, " 'You shall love the LORD your God with all your heart, and with all your soul, and with all your mind.' This is the greatest and first commandment."

MATTHEW 22:35–38

A BBA GREGORY said, "God expects three things of all who are baptized:

Keep the true faith with all your soul and all your strength.

Control your tongue.

Be chaste with your body."

Love the Lord your God.

Can God spread a table in the wilderness?
    PSALM 78:19

PALLADIUS wrote, "An elderly merchant named Apollonius renounced the world and moved to Mount Nitria. Because of his age, he was not able to practice the austere way of life followed by others. Instead, he used his own labor and resources to purchase all kinds of food and medicine in Alexandria. He distributed these to all the monasteries, walking from door to door, looking for the sick. He carried raisins, pomegranates, eggs, and wheat flour. This was his unique ministry for Christ in his old age. As he neared death, he turned over all of his supplies to another, asking him to take care of the five thousand monks living on the mountain. Without this attention, many would not survive in such a desolate place."

Can God spread a table in the wilderness?

23 OCTOBER

On that day, says the LORD, you will call me,
"My husband," and no longer will you call me, "My Baal."
HOSEA 2:16

EVAGRIUS PONTICUS wrote, "Your spirit may avoid becoming emotionally entangled with thoughts about physical things, but this does not guarantee you will achieve true prayer. Thoughts of the hidden nature of things and circumstances may distract you and waste your time. It does not matter that passions do not disturb you when you contemplate them. They remain earthly things that contribute outline and form, directing you far away from God."

Thoughts of the hidden nature
of things may distract you.

Prove me, O LORD, and try me; test my heart and mind.
For your steadfast love is before my eyes,
and I walk in faithfulness to you.
PSALM 26:2–3

WHEN ABBA POEMEN prepared to attend a prayer meeting, he began by sitting alone for an hour of self-examination. Then he would go.

Prove me, O Lord, and try me.

Be doers of the word,
and not merely hearers.
JAMES 1:22

SOME BROTHERS VISITED ABBA ANTONY and asked him to tell them how they could find personal salvation. The old man said, "You are familiar with the Scriptures. That should teach you enough."

"Yes, but we want a word from you also, Abba."

Then the old man responded, "The Gospel instructs you to turn the other cheek."

They said, "We can't do that."

"Then if you can't offer the other cheek, at least permit one cheek to be struck."

They replied, "We can't do that either."

"If these things are beyond you, then do not return evil for evil."

"We can't."

Abba Antony turned to his disciple. "Prepare a little corn chowder for these people, because they are not capable of doing anything." To his visitors he said, "If you can't do this or that, there is nothing I can do for you.

"What you need is prayer."

**Be doers of the word,
and not merely hearers.**

*I am the Alpha and the Omega, the beginning and the end.
To the thirsty I will give water as a gift from the spring of the
water of life. Those who conquer will inherit these things, and I
will be their God and they will be my children.*

REVELATION 21:6–7

ABBA JOHN went to see Abba Paesius, who had lived in a remote part of the desert for forty years. With genuine respect, he asked, "You have lived a solitary life for a long time. Not many troubles could have come your way. Tell me, what progress have you made?"

Paesius said, "Since the day I began my hermitage, I have never eaten during daylight."

John, recalling his years as a solitary, replied, "Neither have I been angry."

Those who conquer will inherit.

You have heard that it was said, "You shall not commit adultery." But I say to you that everyone who looks at a woman with lust has already committed adultery with her in his heart.

MATTHEW 5:27–28

ABBA GERONTIUS OF PETRA said, "Many who are tempted by earthly pleasures do not sin with their bodies, but lust with their minds. Maintaining physical virginity, their hearts are lustful. It is much better to do what is written and closely guard your heart."

Closely guard your heart.

Can you find out the deep things of God? Can you find out the
limit of the Almighty? It is higher than heaven—what can you
do? Deeper than Sheol—what can you know? Its measure is
longer than the earth, and broader than the sea.

JOB 11:7–9

EVAGRIUS PONTICUS wrote, "The profoundest moment of prayer remains susceptible to spiritual misdirection. Perhaps you experience a strange, extraordinary vision. This may mislead you into believing that you know the precise location of God. The abruptness of the revelation allows you to think quantitatively of God, but God is beyond physical quantity and has no outward form."

Can you find out the limit of the Almighty?

The disciples of John came to him [Jesus], saying, "Why do we
and the Pharisees fast often, but your disciples do not fast?"
MATTHEW 9:14

JOSEPH ASKED ABBA POEMEN the best way to fast. Poemen said, "Everyone should eat a little less than he wants, every day."

Joseph said to him, "But when you were a young man, you would sometimes fast two days in a row."

"That's true. Sometimes I would fast three days in a row, or an entire week. But the great hermits have tested all of these things. They discovered that it's best to eat something every day, and then on certain days, a little less."

Eat something every day,
and then on certain days, a little less.

If there is among you anyone in need, a member of your
community in any of your towns within the land that the
LORD your God is giving you, do not be hard-hearted or
tight-fisted toward your needy neighbor.
You should rather open your hand, willingly
lending enough to meet the need, whatever it may be.
DEUTERONOMY 15:7–8

BEFORE A CERTAIN OLD MAN moved into the monastery at Cuziba, it was his custom to help the poor in his village. If he learned of someone who could not afford to sow his field, he would take seed at night, when no one could see him, and sow the poor man's field. The owner knew nothing of it until the seed sprouted.

Open your hand willingly.

Since we have these promises, beloved, let us cleanse ourselves
from every defilement of body and of spirit,
making holiness perfect in the fear of God.
2 CORINTHIANS 7:1

A HERMIT often said, "It is impossible for you to see your face in muddy water. Similarly, the soul is not able to contemplate God in prayer until it is cleansed of destructive thoughts."

Beloved, let us cleanse ourselves.

I have been young, and now am old, yet I have not seen the
righteous forsaken or their children begging bread.
PSALM 37:25

A BENEVOLENT PERSON offered a leprous hermit some money. "You are an old, sick man. Use this money for yourself."

He responded, "Do you want to take me away from God, who has fed me for sixty years? I have been sick all that time, but I have never needed anything that God did not provide." Saying that, the hermit refused to accept the gift.

God will provide.

One who spares words is knowledgeable;
one who is cool in spirit has understanding.
Even fools who keep silent are considered wise;
when they close their lips,
they are deemed intelligent.
PROVERBS 17:27–28

ABBA AGATHON kept a stone in his mouth for three years, until he learned how to keep silent.

Learn how to keep silent.

Those who are wise understand these things;
those who are discerning know them.
HOSEA 14:9

A BROTHER who had committed a serious sin decided to confess it to another monk. Instead of openly stating what he had done, the brother asked, "If a thought like this came into someone's mind, would he be saved?" The monk told him, "There is no hope for you." Hearing this, the brother thought, "If I am going to perish, I might as well do it in the world."

As he was abandoning the solitary life, the brother thought of Abba Silvanus and turned aside to visit him. Again, without reporting the nature of his sin, he asked the same oblique question. Silvanus quoted Scripture and said, "That judgment falls on everyone, whether or not they have sinned." This moved the brother to confess his sin. Like a skilled physician, Silvanus applied an ointment of Scripture texts to the wounded one, observing that repentance is available for everyone who turns to God.

Years later, Silvanus encountered the monk who had discouraged the brother. "That brother, who was crushed by your response and was returning to the world, is now a bright star among us."

Those who are wise understand these things.

I think of you on my bed,
and meditate on you in the watches of the night;
for you have been my help,
and in the shadow of your wings I sing for joy.
My soul clings to you; your right hand upholds me.

PSALM 63:6–8

ABBA JOHN once braided enough rope for the construction of two baskets, but he wove it all into one basket. He did not notice what he was doing until he attempted to hang it up, because his mind was preoccupied with the contemplation of God.

My soul clings to God.

5 NOVEMBER

It is always good to give your attention to something worthwhile, even when I am not with you.
GALATIANS 4:18 CEV

ABBA MOSES asked ABBA SILVANUS if a monk could live every day with the same enthusiasm he experienced on the first day of his monastic life. Silvanus replied, "If you are genuinely committed to your choice of life, you can live every day, every hour, as it was when you began your life as a monk."

Live every day as it was when you began.

Do nothing from selfish ambition or conceit, but in humility
regard others as better than yourselves.

PHILIPPIANS 2:3

ABBA POEMEN said, "In the same way our nostrils inhale air, we should constantly absorb humility and reverence for God."

Constantly absorb humility and reverence.

7 NOVEMBER

He makes a god and worships it,
*   makes it a carved image*
*   and bows down before it.*
            ISAIAH 44:15

EVAGRIUS PONTICUS wrote, "When you pray, do not attempt to imagine the form of the Divinity. Do not allow your spirit to dwell on any image. Free yourself from all material pictures as you draw near the immaterial Being. Your spiritual understanding will improve."

**When you pray,
do not imagine the form of the Divinity.**

8 NOVEMBER

When his brothers saw that their father loved him more than
all his brothers, they hated him,
and could not speak peaceably to him.

GENESIS 37:4

As JOHN THE DWARF sat in front of the church, a group of brothers clustered around him, seeking his opinion of their ideas. Another hermit observed this and became jealous of their attention. He said, "John, your cup is filled with poison."

"Yes, Abba," John answered. "It is. But you have only seen the outside. What would you say if you could see the inside?"

You have only seen the outside.
What would you say if you could see the inside?

The LORD your God you shall fear; him you shall serve,
and by his name alone you shall swear.

DEUTERONOMY 6:13

EVAGRIUS PONTICUS wrote, "When you pray, you stand before the omnipotent God, Creator and Provider of everything. How can you fail to respect and revere God who is beyond all measure, even as you fear instead mosquitoes and roaches? Pay attention to what Moses tells you, 'The Lord your God you shall fear.'"

The Lord your God you shall fear.

Someone will say, "You have faith and I have works."
Show me your faith apart from your works,
and I by my works will show you my faith.
JAMES 2:18

A BBA POEMEN said, "Teach your heart to follow what your tongue speaks to others. We attempt to appear excellent in our preaching, but we are less than excellent in practicing what we preach."

I by my works will show you my faith.

I desire, then, that in every place the men should pray, lifting up holy hands without anger or argument.

1 TIMOTHY 2:8

A GROUP OF BROTHERS visited some hermits in the desert. After a prayer and introductions, they sat down together for conversation. When they were ready to leave, they requested more prayers. One of the hermits asked, "Haven't you already prayed?"

"Yes, Abba," one of the brothers answered, "when we entered, we prayed, but since then we have been talking."

The hermit said, "Perhaps I am mistaken, brothers, but one of you, while we were sitting and talking, offered a hundred and three prayers." Then they prayed again and departed.

Pray, lifting up holy hands.

Has the LORD as great delight in burnt offerings and sacrifices, as in obedience to the voice of the LORD? Surely, to obey is better than sacrifice, and to heed than the fat of rams.
1 SAMUEL 15:22

A BBA HYPERICHIUS said, "A monk's service is obedience. One who is obedient will have answered prayers and stand beside the Crucified in sure faith. This is the way our Lord went to his cross—obedient unto death."

To obey is better than sacrifice.

Do not put yourself forward in the king's presence or stand in
the place of the great; for it is better to be told, "Come up here,"
than to be put lower in the presence of a noble.

PROVERBS 25:6–7

A BROTHER ASKED POEMEN, "How should I conduct myself in the place where I live?"

Poemen answered, "Be as careful as a stranger, and wherever you are, do not expect the things you say to be taken seriously. Do this and you will discover peace."

Do not expect to be taken seriously.

14 NOVEMBER

Let us celebrate the festival, not with the old yeast,

the yeast of malice and evil,

but with the unleavened bread of sincerity and truth.

1 CORINTHIANS 5:8

ABBA ZOSIMAS said, "There is power in the words of the elders. Their comments came from experience and truth, as holy Antony observed. Their words carry weight because they personally practiced what they recommended. As one of the sages expressed it, 'Let your words be confirmed by your life.'"

Let your words be confirmed by your life.

They had argued with one another who was the greatest.
MARK 9:34

FOR MANY YEARS, TWO HERMITS lived together without any conflict or disagreement. One suggested they have a quarrel to see how others live. The other answered, "I don't know how to start a quarrel."

The first said, "Look, I'll put this brick on the ground between us and claim it is mine. Then you insist it belongs to you. That's how quarrels begin."

They put the brick between them. One said, "That's mine." The other said, "No, that's mine." The first answered, "Yes, it belongs to you. Take it." They were not able to argue with each other.

**Live together without any
conflict or disagreement.**

Are you able to drink the cup that I am about to drink?
MATTHEW 20:22

AMMA DIONYSIA gave alms to a beggar, but less than he wanted. The beggar began to speak harshly to her, and Dionysia took offense, wanting to strike back.

Abba Zosimas corrected her, saying, "You are striking against yourself. You are chasing every virtue from your soul. Can you endure what Christ endured? My lady, I know that you have given away your possessions as though they had no value. But until you become meek, you are like a metal smith pounding a bar of iron and failing to produce a useful object. You will know you have become meek when insults no longer annoy you."

**Are you able to drink the cup
that I am about to drink?**

The night is far gone, the day is near. Let us then lay aside the works of darkness and put on the armor of light; let us live honorably as in the day. ROMANS 13:12–13

ABBA PHILAGRIUS lived in Jerusalem and with much labor managed to earn enough to eat. When he was selling his crafts in the market place, someone accidentally dropped a bag of coins near him. Philagrius found it and thought, "The one who lost this will soon return looking for it."

It wasn't long before the distressed man came back. Philagrius took him aside and returned his coin pouch. The relieved owner offered to give him some of the money as a reward, but the hermit refused to accept anything. The owner began to shout, "Come see what this man of God is like!" Philagrius slipped quietly away and left town before anyone could praise him for what he had done.

Let us live honorably as in the day.

This is our boast, the testimony of our conscience: we have behaved in the world with frankness and godly sincerity, not by earthly wisdom but by the grace of God.

2 CORINTHIANS 1:12

AMMON OF RAITHU VISITED ABBA SISOIS. He told him, "When I read Scripture, I think it is important to prepare sophisticated commentaries in order to answer questions about it."

Sisois replied, "That is not necessary. It is better to speak simply, with a clean conscience and a pure mind."

Speak simply.

As they came from their mother's womb, so they shall go again,
naked as they came; they shall take nothing for their toil, which
they may carry away with their hands.

ECCLESIASTES 5:15

ABBA ZOSIMAS would pick up small objects such as a nail, a short thread, and other valueless castoffs. He would ask, "Would you fight or argue over this? Would you harbor a grudge or get sick over this? That would be insanity. Anyone who is making progress in God can think of the entire world as this nail, no matter how much of the world he possesses. There is no harm in owning something, but trouble comes when we are attached to what we own."

**Trouble comes
when we are attached to what we own.**

People are slaves to whatever masters them.

2 PETER 2:19

ABBA ZOSIMAS said, "A person may be indifferent to large amounts of money, but be obsessively attached to a small needle. The needle becomes more valuable than the money. In this way, one can become a slave of the needle, or a monk's cap, or a handkerchief, or a book, instead of being God's servant."

People are slaves to whatever masters them.

To the present hour we are hungry and thirsty, we are poorly
clothed and beaten and homeless, and we grow weary from
the work of our own hands. When reviled, we bless; when
persecuted, we endure; when slandered, we speak kindly.
We have become like the rubbish of the world,
the dregs of all things, to this very day.
1 CORINTHIANS 4:11–13

AMMA SYNCLETICA said, "You cannot build a ship without nails, and you can't be saved without humility."

When reviled, we bless.

The LORD will guide you continually.
ISAIAH 58:11

EVAGRIUS said, "The best cures for a wandering mind are reading and prayer. Hunger, labor, and solitude reduce passion. Psalmody, patience, and mercy control anger. All of these remedies have a proper time and amount. If you practice them at inappropriate times and excessively, they may briefly do a little good. But what helps you for a little while may be destructive over longer time."

The Lord will guide you continually.

23 NOVEMBER

We destroy arguments and every proud obstacle
raised up against the knowledge of God,
and we take every thought
captive to obey Christ.
2 CORINTHIANS 10:4–5

ABBA ISAIAH ASKED ABBA POEMEN about dealing with impure thoughts. Poemen responded, "If you leave cloth closed in a chest for a long time, it will decay. If you do not allow those thoughts to emerge into action, they will eventually rot."

Take every thought captive to obey Christ.

Rejoice, even if now for a little while you have had to suffer
various trials, so that the genuineness of your faith—being
more precious than gold that, though perishable, is tested by
fire—may be found to result in praise and glory and honor
when Jesus Christ is revealed.

1 PETER 1:6–7

ABBA ZOSIMAS said, "There is no way to become holy without tempting thoughts. Evade valuable temptation and you will evade eternal life. A saint pointed out that their persecutors presented crowns to martyrs. Those who stoned Stephen glorified him. I agree with Evagrius, anyone who accuses me is my benefactor. Dishonor is medicine for a self-centered soul."

Rejoice even if now you suffer various trials.

Since he would not be persuaded,
we remained silent except to say,
"The Lord's will be done."
ACTS 21:14

EVAGRIUS PONTICUS wrote, "Instead of setting your heart on what seems good to you, seek what is pleasing to God when you pray. This will prevent agitation and allow you to focus on thanksgiving when you pray."

The Lord's will be done.

26 NOVEMBER

Those who eat, eat in honor of the Lord,
since they give thanks to God; while those who abstain,
abstain in honor of the LORD and give thanks to God.

ROMANS 14:6

ABBA NILUS said, "Have no desire for things to be as you prefer. If you desire only what pleases God, you will be spared confusion and your prayers will be of thanksgiving."

Do everything in honor of the Lord.

When he had taken the scroll, the four living creatures
and the twenty-four elders fell before the Lamb,
each holding a harp and golden bowls full of incense,
which are the prayers of the saints.
REVELATION 5:8

EVAGRIUS PONTICUS wrote:
Prayer is the beautiful blossoming of gentleness and warmth.

Prayer is the fruit of happiness and thanksgiving.

Prayer is the elimination of melancholy and dejection.

Prayer is the rise of our spirit to God.

When you immerse yourself in prayer, ascend above all other delights and you will discover true prayer.

Prayer is the rise of our spirit to God.

If you love those who love you, what reward do you have? Do
not even the tax collectors do the same? And if you greet only
your brothers and sisters, what more are you doing than others?
Do not even the Gentiles do the same?

MATTHEW 5:46–47

A BROTHER TOLD A HERMIT, "I will not invite anyone
who is known to be guilty of sin into my cell. A
good person is always welcomed."

The hermit replied, "If you do good for a good person,
that makes no difference to him. Give the sinner twice as
much love, because he is sick."

Give the sinner twice as much love.

How sweet are your words to my taste,

sweeter than honey to my mouth!

Through your precepts I get understanding;

therefore I hate every false way.

PSALM 119:103–104

ABBA ZOSIMAS enjoyed reading the sayings of the Holy Fathers. For him, they were like the air he breathed. From them, he obtained the best fruit of all the virtues.

How sweet are your words.

30 NOVEMBER

Jesus said to them, "Come and have breakfast."
JOHN 21:12

ON A FEAST DAY IN CELLIA, brothers gathered to eat a meal at church. One of them told a server, "I do not eat anything that has been cooked. I only eat salted food."

The server called out to another, "This brother does not eat cooked food! Bring him some salt!"

One of the brothers told the one on the restricted diet, "You would have done better to eat meat alone in your cell today than to have had this announced in front of everyone."

Come and have breakfast.

And going a little farther, he [Jesus]
threw himself on the ground and prayed,
"My Father, if it is possible, let this cup pass from me;
yet not what I want but what you want."
MATTHEW 26:39

EVAGRIUS PONTICUS wrote, "Often in my prayers I kept asking God for what I thought was good. I repeatedly made personal requests, unreasonably coercing God. I was not able to trust God's providence to work things out for my best interests. When I got what I sought, I was sorry that I had insisted on my own desires. Things did not turn out the way I had imagined."

Not what I want, but what you, Father, want.

2 DECEMBER

O LORD God of hosts, who is as mighty as you, O LORD?
Your faithfulness surrounds you. You rule the raging of the sea;
when its waves rise, you still them.

PSALM 89:8–9

THALASSIOS THE LIBYAN said, "Subdue your senses by stillness. Be firm with the thoughts that create a noisy commotion in your heart."

God rules the raging sea.

3 DECEMBER

Strive to enter through the narrow door; for many,
I tell you, will try to enter and will not be able.

LUKE 13:24

ABBA AMMONAS said, "When Christ mentioned the narrow door, he meant controlling your thoughts and eliminating your own will, for the sake of God. This is also the meaning of Christ's disciples in Matthew's Gospel, 'We have left everything and followed you.'"

Strive to enter through the narrow door.

Beware that you are not carried away with the error of the lawless and lose your own stability. But grow in the grace and knowledge of our Lord and Savior Jesus Christ.

2 PETER 3:17–18

AMMA SYNCLETICA said, "If you live in a monastic community, it would be harmful for you to move from one place to another. If a hen gets off her nest and stops brooding her eggs, she will hatch no chickens. Move frequently from one religious location to another and your faith will grow cold."

Grow in the grace and knowledge of our Lord.

Ho, everyone who thirsts, come to the waters; and you that have no money, come, buy and eat! Come, buy wine and milk without money and without price. Why do you spend your money for that which is not bread, and your labor for that which does not satisfy? Listen carefully to me, and eat what is good, and delight yourselves in rich food. Incline your ear, and come to me; listen, so that you may live.

ISAIAH 55:1–3

ABBA EPIPHANIUS said, "God sells righteousness at a bargain price to those who are interested: a scrap of bread, a cheap cloak, a cup of cool water, a tiny coin."

Incline your ear, and come to me.

6 DECEMBER

Who shall ascend the hill of the LORD? And who shall stand
in his holy place? Those who have clean hands and pure hearts,
who do not lift up their souls to what is false,
and do not swear deceitfully.

PSALM 24:3–4

EVAGRIUS PONTICUS wrote, "Notice whether or not you are truly in God's presence when you pray. It could be that you are looking for recognition and approval from other people. If this is your motivation for prayer, it is a hollow prayer."

Do not lift up your soul to what is false.

One thing I asked of the LORD, that will I seek after: to live in the house of the LORD all the days of my life, to behold the beauty of the LORD, and to inquire in his temple.

PSALM 27:4

PAMBO ASKED ABBA ANTONY, "What shall I do?" Antony told him, "Avoid self-righteousness. Do not grieve past sins interminably. Control your tongue and your appetite."

Live in the house of the Lord.

Do to others as you would have them do to you.

LUKE 6:31

DESERT HERMITS taught, "If there is any behavior you dislike in others, avoid it yourself. If you do not like receiving criticism, do not criticize another person. If slander upsets you, do not slander anyone. If you are troubled by aggressive, demeaning people, do not behave that way yourself."

**If there is any behavior you dislike,
do not do that to someone else.**

The conspirators came and found Daniel praying and seeking
mercy before his God. Then they approached the king and said,
". . . Daniel, one of the exiles from Judah, pays no attention to
you, O king, or to the interdict you have signed,
but he is saying his prayers three times a day."
DANIEL 6:11–13

A BROTHER ASKED ABBA POEMEN, "How should we live?"

Poemen replied, "Daniel is an excellent example. The only charge his accusers could bring against him was that he served his God."

Serve God.

Love your enemies, do good to those who hate you, bless those who curse you, pray for those who abuse you. If anyone strikes you on the cheek, offer the other also; and from anyone who takes away your coat do not withhold even your shirt. Give to everyone who begs from you; and if anyone takes away your goods, do not ask for them again.

LUKE 6:27–30

ABBA SISOIS said, "Let others despise you. Put your own will behind you. Place yourself beyond worldly interests. Accomplish these things and you will have peace."

Love your enemies.

You have no delight in sacrifice; if I were to give a burnt offering, you would not be pleased. The sacrifice acceptable to God is a broken spirit; a broken and contrite heart, O God, you will not despise.

PSALM 51:16–17

A DESERT HERMIT said, "As our bodies are always accompanied by a shadow, let us take penitence and lamentation with us everywhere."

God will not despise a contrite heart.

In those times it was not safe for anyone to go or come, for great
disturbances afflicted all the inhabitants of the lands. They were
broken in pieces, nation against nation and city against city,
for God troubled them with every sort of distress. But you, take
courage! Do not let your hands be weak,
for your work shall be rewarded.
2 CHRONICLES 15:5–7

EVAGRIUS told about a hermit who said, "I eliminate physical pleasure in order to eliminate opportunities to become angry. I understand that my struggle with anger is the result of desiring pleasure. Anger disturbs my mind and disorders my thoughts."

Anger disturbs one's mind.

Now to him who by the power at work within us is able
to accomplish abundantly far more than all we can ask or
imagine, to him be glory in the church and in Christ Jesus to all
generations, forever and ever. Amen.

EPHESIANS 3:20–21

EVAGRIUS PONTICUS wrote, "Do not be distressed by delayed answers to your prayers. The Lord wants to give you more than you ask, and will reward your patience in prayer. What could be better than to be in intimate conversation with God and to be absorbed in him?"

What is better than
intimate conversation with God?

Pursue righteousness, godliness, faith,
love, endurance, gentleness.

TIMOTHY 6:11

ABBA HILARION received an invitation from Epiphanius, the bishop from Cyprus, who wanted to see the hermit before he died. Once they had greeted each other, others placed a piece of chicken in front of them. The bishop picked it up and offered it to Hilarion, but the hermit declined to accept it, saying, "Since I became a monk, I have not eaten meat."

Epiphanius responded, "Since I put on the habit, I have not let anyone go to sleep who continued to hold something against me, and I have never gone to bed aware of any enemy in the world."

Hilarion humbly acknowledged, "Your devotion is greater than mine."

Pursue righteousness.

If you forgive others their trespasses, your heavenly Father will also forgive you; but if you do not forgive others, neither will your Father forgive your trespasses.

MATTHEW 6:14–15

A PHRAHAT THE PERSIAN said, "Prayer is a lovely thing with glowing results. Good works must accompany prayer for it to be acceptable to God. God hears prayer when it rises out of a forgiving spirit. God always answers pure and sincere prayer. Prayer becomes potent when God's energy permeates it."

God hears prayer
when it rises out of a forgiving spirit.

The people who walked in darkness have seen a great light;
those who lived in a land of deep darkness—
on them light has shined.

ISAIAH 9:2

BROTHER JOHN KLIMAKOS said, "If a sunbeam penetrates a house through a crack, it sheds light on what is inside, revealing even floating particles of dust. Reverence for God works the same way. When the fear of the Lord enters us, it discloses all the imperfection remaining in us."

The people who walked in darkness
have seen a great light.

You have heard that it was said, "You shall love your neighbor and hate your enemy." But I say to you, Love your enemies and pray for those who persecute you.

MATTHEW 5:43–44

EVAGRIUS PONTICUS wrote, "If you harbor grievances and offenses and yet think you are praying, you are doing nothing more than drawing water from a well and pouring it into a bucket that is full of holes."

Prayer has no room for grievances.

If I find favor with you, do not pass by your servant. Let a
little water be brought, and wash your feet, and rest yourselves
under the tree. Let me bring a little bread, that you may refresh
yourselves, and after that you may pass on.

GENESIS 18:3–5

THEODORUS THE ASCETIC said, "The patriarch Abraham offered hospitality to everyone who passed by his tent, even the bad-mannered and undeserving. Because of this, he also entertained God's angels. If we practice unconditional hospitality, we may welcome not only angels, but also the Lord himself. Jesus told us, 'As you did it to one of the least of these who are members of my family, you did it to me' (Matthew 25:40). It is good to be kind to everyone, especially anyone who is not able to repay you."

It is good to be kind to everyone.

Do you not know that you are God's temple
and that God's Spirit dwells in you?
1 CORINTHIANS 3:16

APHRAHAT THE PERSIAN ascetic said, "Our Lord instructed us to pray in secret, by which he means in your heart. He also told us to close the door. The door we must shut is the mouth. We are Christ's temple, as the Apostle said, and the Lord enters your inner self in this temple. Christ will purge it of any uncleanliness, but only while the door (your mouth) is shut."

God's Spirit dwells in you.

20 DECEMBER

If you indeed cry out for insight, and raise your voice for understanding; if you seek it like silver, and search for it as for hidden treasures—then you will understand the fear of the LORD and find the knowledge of God.
PROVERBS 2:3–5

A BROTHER asked a hermit how the fear of God comes into the soul. He answered, "If you are humble and live in poverty, making no judgment of others, fear of God will be present in you."

Understand the fear of the Lord.

Make me understand the way of your precepts, and I will
meditate on your wondrous works.
PSALM 119:27

DIADOCHOS OF PHOTIKE said, "An uninspired person should not attempt to speculate on spiritual mysteries. When the Holy Spirit sheds a flood of light, the one who receives it should not attempt to express it in words. A soul intoxicated with divine love will enjoy God's glory in silence."

I will meditate on your wondrous works.

A man named Ananias, with the consent of his wife Sapphira,
sold a piece of property; with his wife's knowledge,
he kept back some of the proceeds, and brought only a part and
laid it at the apostles' feet.

ACTS 5:1–2

CASSIAN reports that Syncleticus turned away from the world, giving his possessions to the poor. Unwilling to embrace total poverty and the expected rule of monastic life, he retained some funds for himself. Basil told him, "You are no longer a senator, but you are not yet a monk."

Withhold nothing.

*Then Mary said, "Here am I, the servant of the Lord; let it be
with me according to your word."* LUKE 1:38

SILVANUS had an obedient disciple in Scetis named
Mark, who copied old manuscripts. The hermit loved
Mark because of his obedience.

Hermits living nearby were disturbed when they
learned Silvanus had a favorite disciple. They visited him
to express their concern. Silvanus took them out of his cell
and began to knock on the door of several of his disciples,
saying, "Brother, come out. I have something for you to
do." They did not respond quickly.

When he knocked at Mark's door, he opened it
immediately and Silvanus sent him on a little errand.
Turning to the visiting delegation, he asked, "Where are
the others?" Then they entered Mark's cell and saw that
he had been copying a book. He was forming the letter O
when he heard Silvanus knock. He had not taken time to
complete the circle.

Here am I, the servant of the Lord.

There was a man sent from God, whose name was John.
He came as a witness to testify to the light,
so that all might believe through him.
He himself was not the light, but he came to testify to the light.
The true light, which enlightens everyone,
was coming into the world.
JOHN 1:6–9

SAHDONA THE SYRIAN said, "The soul is blessed when its eye no longer sees all the dark storm clouds of sorrows of the present time. Instead, it sees, clearly and simply, the Lord wrapped in an aura of light."

The true light was coming into the world.

With all wisdom and insight he has made known to us the
mystery of his will, according to his good pleasure that he set
forth in Christ, as a plan for the fullness of time, to gather up
all things in him, things in heaven and things on earth.
EPHESIANS 1:8–10

BASIL OF CÆSAREA contributed to an ancient liturgy. "You have visited us in many ways because of your love and kindness. You sent the prophets and worked mighty wonders through the saints who, from generation to generation, were close to you. . . . You helped us with your gift of the Law. You direct your angels to watch over us. When the fullness of time had come, you spoke to us by your own Son."

He has made known to us the mystery of his will.

> *When you are disturbed, do not sin;*
> *ponder it on your beds, and be silent.*
> *Offer right sacrifices,*
> *and put your trust in the LORD.*
>
> PSALM 4:4–5

BROTHER JOHN KLIMAKOS said, "Stillness in the soul is continual worship of God, being present in the divine presence. If an awareness of the name of Jesus comes with every breath, you will discover the importance of being still."

Be still, and put your trust in the Lord.

Out of the mouths of infants and nursing babies you have
prepared praise for yourself.
MATTHEW 21:16

DOROTHEOS OF GAZA said, "If you sincerely want to do the will of God with all your heart, God will never abandon you. God will guide you along the path of his will. If you truly seek God's will, God will use even a little child as a means of communication. On the other hand, if you are not honestly seeking to know and do the will of God, not even a prophet would be able to direct you."

God will guide you along the path of his will.

Why are you cast down, O my soul,
and why are you disquieted within me? Hope in God;
for I shall again praise him, my help and my God.
PSALM 42:5–6

JOHN OF KARPATHOS said, "God's grace will occasionally brightly illuminate some people for a while, but then dissipate. Such a person may become depressed, begin to grumble, and even abandon any effort at prayer instead of giving it renewed energy. This is like an ungrateful beggar, seeking alms at the palace door, who walks away indignantly because he did not receive an invitation to dine with the king."

Hope in God.

The son said to him, "Father, I have sinned against heaven and
before you; I am no longer worthy to be called your son." But the
father said to his slaves, "Quickly, bring out a robe—the best
one—and put it on him; put a ring on his finger
and sandals on his feet."
LUKE 15:21–22

BROTHER JOHN KLIMAKOS said, "Keep your prayers completely simple. Both the tax collector and the prodigal son were reconciled to God when they spoke one simple idea. The tax collector said, 'God, be merciful to me, a sinner' (Luke 18:13). The prodigal son said, 'Father, I have sinned against heaven and before you' (Luke 15:21)."

God, be merciful to me, a sinner.

How can you say to your neighbor,
"Let me take the speck out of your eye,"
while the log is in your own eye?
You hypocrite, first take the log out of your own eye,
and then you will see clearly
to take the speck out of your neighbor's eye.
MATTHEW 7:4–5

A N EGYPTIAN ABBA said, "Never judge anyone, for any reason. Never do anyone harm. Discipline yourself, purging both material and spiritual evil. Nurture a modest and gentle spirit. Do these things, noticing your own faults rather than those of others, and the grace of our Lord Jesus Christ will be with you lavishly."

Never judge anyone, for any reason.

I will seek the lost, and I will bring back the strayed, and I will bind up the injured, and I will strengthen the weak.

EZEKIEL 34:16

A MONK VISITED ABBA SISOES and told him he had fallen from grace. "What should I do, Abba?"

Sisoes replied, "Get up again."

After a while, the monk returned to ask, "What can I do now? For I have fallen again."

"Get up again," the old man said to him, "Never stop getting up again."

Never stop getting up again.

ABOUT PARACLETE PRESS

WHO WE ARE

Paraclete Press is an ecumenical publisher of books and recordings on Christian spirituality. Our publishing represents a full expression of Christian belief and practice—from Catholic to Evangelical, from Protestant to Orthodox.

Paraclete Press is the publishing arm of the Community of Jesus, an ecumenical monastic community in the Benedictine tradition. As such, we are uniquely positioned in the marketplace without connection to a large corporation and with informal relationships to many branches and denominations of faith.

We like it best when people buy our books from booksellers, our partners in successfully reaching as wide an audience as possible.

WHAT WE ARE DOING

Books

Paraclete Press publishes books that show the richness and depth of what it means to be Christian. Although Benedictine spirituality is at the heart of all that we do, we publish books that reflect the Christian experience across many cultures, time periods, and houses of worship.

We publish books that nourish the vibrant life of the church and its people—books about spiritual practice, formation, history, ideas, and customs.

We have several different series of books within Paraclete Press, including the best-selling Living Library series of modernized classic texts; A Voice from the Monastery—giving voice to men and women monastics about what it means to live a spiritual life today; award-winning literary faith fiction; and books that explore Judaism and Islam and discover how these faiths inform Christian thought and practice.

Recordings

From Gregorian chant to contemporary American choral works, our music recordings celebrate the richness of sacred choral music through the centuries. Paraclete is proud to distribute the recordings of the internationally acclaimed choir Gloriæ Dei Cantores, who have been praised for their "rapt and fathomless spiritual intensity" by *American Record Guide*, and the Gloriæ Dei Cantores Schola, which specializes in the study and performance of Gregorian chant. Paraclete is also the exclusive North American distributor of the recordings of the Monastic Choir of St. Peter's Abbey in Solesmes, France, long considered to be a leading authority on Gregorian chant performance.

Learn more about us at our Web site:
www.paracletepress.com, or call us toll-free at 1-800-451-5006.

If you liked *By Way of the Desert*, you may also enjoy:

Incandescence

ISBN: 978-1-55725-418-4
276 pages, $16.95, trade paper

Incandescence offers fresh translations from the writings of famous and not-so-famous mystics—Julian of Norwich, Mechthild of Magdeburg, Catherine of Siena, Hildegard of Bingen, Gertrude of Helfta, Margery Kempe, and others. Each reading includes a meditation, prayer, poem, or song, offering stunning insights into God's divine, mothering love, the guidance of God's light, the sensuality of faith, and more.

Nearer to the Heart of God

ISBN: 978-1-55725-417-6
399 pages, $17.95, trade paper

These timeless devotional readings are culled from the classic works of some of the best-loved Christian authors. Each reading beautifully expresses the heart of the Christian way, with all its challenges and possibilities.